Mary Stuart

Friedrich von Schiller remains one of Germany's most influential poets and dramatists. He was born in Württemberg in 1759 and had his first success with the production of *Die Räuber* in 1782 which gained him instant artistic success. His most successful and popular works include his first historical tragedy, *Don Carlos* (1789), and his great dramatic trilogy, *Wallenstein*, completed in 1799. Schiller also enjoyed a friendship and professional collaboration with Goethe, this relationship leading to many of Schiller's most revered works – *Maria Stuart* (1800), *Die Jungfrau von Orleans* (1801), *Die Braut von Messina* (1803) and *Wilhelm Tell* (1804). Despite his professional success, Schiller suffered serious financial debt as a young man and in 1805 he died, aged 46, from tuberculosis. All his plays have been translated into English.

Mike Poulton began writing for the theatre in 1995. His first two productions, *Uncle Vanya* and *Fortune's Fool*, were staged the following year at the Chichester Festival Theatre. Since then, productions have included *The Lady from the Sea* (Birmingham Rep), *The Cherry Orchard* (Clwyd Theatr Cymru), *The Canterbury Tales* in two parts (RSC), *The Father* (Chichester's Minerva Theatre), and *Uncle Vanya* (Broadway). Other productions include *The Dance of Death* and Euripides' *Ion* (Mercury Theatre, Colchester), *Ghosts* (Plymouth Theatre Royal), *St Erkenwald* (RSC) and *Three Sisters* (Birmingham Rep).

In 2005 Poulton's adaptation of Schiller's *Don Carlos* (Sheffield Crucible and West End) won an Olivier Award. In 2003 his play *Fortune's Fool* was produced on Broadway and went on to win seven major awards including the Tony for Best Actor for Alan Bates, and the Tony for Best Featured Actor for Frank Langella. In 2001 his adaptation of the *York Mystery Plays* was performed for the first time in York Minster.

Friedrich von Schiller

Mary Stuart

a version by
Mike Poulton

Methuen Drama

Published by Methuen Drama 2009

1 3 5 7 9 10 8 6 4 2

Methuen Drama
A & C Black Publishers Limited
36 Soho Square
London W1D 3QY
www.methuendrama.com

ISBN: 978 1 408 19993 0

A CIP catalogue record for this book is available from the British Library

Typeset by Country Setting, Kingsdown, Kent

This version of *Mary Stuart* was first performed at Clwyd Theatr Cymru on 7 May 2009. The cast was as follows:

Margaret Kurl	Catrin Aaron
Count Aubespine/Captain	Wayne Cater
Sir Amyas Paulet	John Cording
Mary Stuart	Marina Hands
Edward Mortimer	Lee Haven-Jones
Robert Melville	Gwyn Vaughan Jones
William Davison	Guy Lewis
Hannah Kennedy	Vivienne Moore
Queen Elizabeth I	Claire Price
Robert Dudley, Earl of Leicester	Steffan Rhodri
George Talbot, Earl of Shrewsbury	Joshua Richards
William Cecil, Lord Burghley	Owen Teale

Director Terry Hands
Designer Max Jones
Composer Colin Towns
Lighting Terry Hands
Sound Matthew Williams

Mary Stuart

Characters

Mary Stuart, *Queen of Scotland*
Elizabeth I, *Queen of England*
William Cecil, Lord Burghley, *Chief Secretary of State to Queen Elizabeth*
Robert Dudley, Earl of Leicester
George Talbot, Earl of Shrewsbury
Henry Grey, Earl of Kent, *the Lord Marshall* +
William Davison, *Queen Elizabeth's secretary* +
Sir Amyas Paulet, *Queen Mary's keeper*
Edward Mortimer, *Paulet's nephew* +
Drugeon Drury, *Paulet's assistant* +
Count Aubespine, *the French Ambassador* +
Count Bellievre, *an emissary from the Duke of Anjou* +
Melville, *Queen Mary's steward* +
Hannah Kennedy, *her nurse*
Margaret Kurl, *a lady-in-waiting to Queen Mary* +
Page, *to Queen Elizabeth* +
Officer, *Captain of Elizabeth's guard* +
True-love's Champion, *a male singer* +
Chastity, *a female singer* +

Other non-speaking parts:

Lust, an actor in the masque; sheriff; Richard Fletcher, Dean of Peterborough; guards; soldiers; huntsmen; ladies-in-waiting; English lords; French lords; servants; singers; actors; etc.

+ Parts marked thus may be doubled.

Act One

Paulet (*bursting in*)
  Axes! Axes!

Paulet *and* **Drury** *watch while two soldiers begin to demolish a cabinet with axes.*

Paulet (*to a third soldier*)
  Pull down that Canopy of State –

Third soldier removes the canopy from above **Mary**'s *chair of state.*

Paulet
  She is no queen – No longer has the right –
  Mary –

Kennedy
  Mother of God!
  What in the names of all the saints above! –

Paulet
  A jewel, Mistress Kennedy – this jewelled pendant –
  Recognise it? – Thrown from a window
  By whom? By you – by her?
  To whom? A gardener? A child? A messenger? –
  Whom do you seek to corrupt?

Kennedy
  Old man –

Paulet
  Have you more? Our searches yield nothing.
  O I believe you're laughing at me! –
  So now we must be thorough! Smash it open!

Kennedy
  Old goat! Old fool! You'll find nothing but papers –

Paulet
  It's papers we're after –

Drury

    And here they are!

The cabinet is demolished revealing boxes of papers and writing materials.
And an ivory box about a foot square.

    These are all in French –

Kennedy

    French is My Lady's mother tongue – witless block!

Drury

    French is the language of the enemy – the language of
        the devil!

Kennedy

    Yes – your own Queen's fluent in it!
    See! Innocent drafts – letters written to Elizabeth –

Paulet

    The Queen shall receive them – spotted and blotted as
        they are.

Enter **Margaret Kurl**

Paulet

    That ivory box –

Drury

    It's locked –

Paulet

    Axes! Axes!

Kurl

    No, sir! No, sir!

Paulet

    See what's inside.

Kurl

    The coronet she wore upon her wedding day –

Drury

    Which wedding day? –

Paulet

She's had so many –

Kurl

A handkerchief
embroidered with the fleurs de lys of France when she was
    France's queen –
Oh sir – of your humanity – leave her some memories –
For pity's sake save something of her past.
In all your coldness never a spark of warmth?

Paulet

An axe.

*They break open the ivory box and find the coronet, handkerchief and one
or two other things of little except sentimental value.*

Drury?

He collects the objects.

Drury

Nothing suspicious – little of value –

Kennedy

Value? How could you judge? To My Lady these are
    everything – all she has left –

Paulet

These objects will be locked away until . . .

Exit **Kurl.**

Paulet

Locked away.

Kennedy

Cold, bare walls.
Are you fit lodging for a princess of the blood –
Once Queen of France, still Scotland's rightful Queen?

Paulet

No, Mistress –

Kennedy

No, indeed, sir, they are not! –

Paulet
No longer Queen –

Kennedy
Where is her Canopy of State, ablaze with stars –
The emblem of the heavens above our heads?

Drury
We've pulled it down –

Kennedy
Where are the woven carpets she should walk upon?
Where is her plate, her furniture, her finery?
All signs of royalty she is denied –
Even her music, and her books are gone –

Drury
What should a woman do with books?

Paulet
She has the English Bible should she need instruction –
Her music was popish lamentation – all screeching
   Ave Marias – superstitious trash!
It sets good Christian teeth on edge to hear them wail.

Kennedy
Base man! Is it not enough, that you strip and pick away
the poor last threads of majesty due to her?
Have you orders to deny her any show of kindness?
Is such harshness – such spite – Elizabeth's, or your own?
Quiet souls find the rewards of solitude even in a prison,
but this mean and petty persecution proclaims Queen
   Mary's keepers less than human.

Paulet
I have denied her the temptations of the world.
She should thank me.
Heaven knows she's had her fill of vanities!
Now she has leisure to examine her blotted conscience.
Let her search her wicked soul –
grovel before God – a wretched penitent –
confessing all her sins –

Kennedy
Oho, well said!
We'll make a Catholic of you yet –

Drury
Now God forbid! –

Kennedy
God will judge her as He will judge us all.
No English court can try a Scottish queen –

Paulet
She shall be judged where she commits her crimes –

Kennedy
What, here in prison?
What crimes may she do here?
Is bare existence now a felony in England?

Drury
Yes! In her case, yes! –

Paulet
Her name incites rebellion.
Satan's unbound! – He's slipped his leash in Rome
and comes to set our Church and State ablaze with heresy.
Legions of fiends flit here from France and settle in the hearts
    of English youth – seduced by her to kill Elizabeth –

Drury
Whom Christ protect! –

Paulet
Whom Heaven preserve –

Kennedy
Whom God forgive!

Paulet
Stubborn old woman! – do you persist?
Can you deny that Parry – Babington – procured by Rome,
    seduced by your Lady – were plotting regicide?

Kennedy
Yes! All lies! Snares, forgeries, and traps! I do deny it –

Paulet

Deny, that Norfolk, poor deluded duke, was lured to the
block of shame – sacrificed to Mary's rank idolatry –

Kennedy

Your Queen beheaded him, not mine!

Paulet

Your Queen should weep to hear how England's youth
shuffle in slow procession to their deaths –
summoned to torments by her Siren call to arms.
O black was the day Our hospitable Lady
welcomed your French infection into her realm!

Kennedy

Welcomed! Hospitable!
Old liar! Rejected and despised – hurried from castle to
keep – kept in darkness!
Mary came here, a suppliant, begging shelter from those
storms
Lord Burghley, and Elizabeth herself, raised in Scotland's
Court.
Dungeons are all My Lady's known of English hospitality.

Drury

Your Lady fled –
over our border, with her husband's blood still reeking on
her hands.
A murderess! Adulteress! – hounded from Scotland –

Paulet

Hunted by justice – cursed and deposed by subjects she'd
abused!
O slippery and sly! She never came for shelter – No!
Having lost two crowns of her own, she came sneaking
here to steal another from her cousin Elizabeth – and
pawn it to the French!

Drury

She came to crack and spill our true religion –
stoop English necks under the rusting yoke of Rome.

Paulet

She came to trouble men's consciences with subtle doubt –
to smash their bodies with treason's racks and chains.

Kennedy

My Lady –

Drury

Let her renounce her claim!

Paulet

Yes, let her renounce her claim to England's throne.
Then see how joyfully Elizabeth would send her home.

Kennedy

You mock our helplessness.
Mary no longer has a home.

Paulet

Then let her thank these strong protecting walls
that shelter her from an angry people – howling to tear her
in pieces.
O, I long to be rid of your Lady! The whole world groans
to rid itself of her!
Pray God her end comes soon!
I'd rather be the keeper of hell's gate than succour such
another prisoner as her.

Oho! See! The devil's loose!
Her Saviour clutched in her claws – who sees the abomination
in her heart?

Enter **Mary** *veiled, holding a crucifix before her.*

Kennedy

Royal Lady!
They've taken everything, everything, everything!

Mary (*putting out her hand*)
Hannah.

Kennedy

There's nothing left of majesty –

Mary

> Come here to me. There is no majesty – none at all – in
>   trifling ornament.
> Gold coronets encrusted with pearl – keepsakes – jewels –
>   are formed of glittering earth.
> But majesty is a thing most precious – fashioned in heaven
>   and granted to few.
> Majesty does not tarnish, cannot be stolen, never is debased
>   by base usage –
> The darker its prison, the more brightly it shines.

She picks up some of the papers.

> We need no axes here, sir. That cabinet had a key –
> I would have given those things you've stolen – and willingly.
> Look. A letter to Elizabeth, my royal cousin – take it.
> But give me your word you'll place it in her hands.
> I'd not have it fall into Lord Burghley's –

Paulet

> Don't school me in my duty, Madame. I know how to direct
>   a letter.

Mary

> It will go to Lord Burghley then.

She breaks the seal and hands it to him.

> Here – read it. Read.
> I beg an audience with Her Majesty – the sister I've never
>   seen. Where's the harm?
> Elizabeth's my only equal – I would speak freely to her –
> Woman to woman – queen to queen – Tudor to Tudor. We'd
>   have no need of men.

Drury

> You've spoken freely to men in the past –
> Too many men, and, many men would say, too freely.

Mary

> I have a second request: I wish to receive the sacrament.
> Through my long imprisonment I've been denied its comforts.

They have taken my kingdom and my freedom –
Now that they are conspiring to take my life I cannot think
    Elizabeth would deny me my hopes of the life to come.

Paulet

I'll send you my own chaplain –

Mary

No! What good are Protestants to me? I have no use for
    make-believe.
I need the true faith – Christ in the chalice – alive in the
    bread –
a priest who speaks with the voice of God. And send me
    a man of law –
it's time to make my will. I feel my flint-cold prison
    darkening into a little grave . . .
I must cherish these remaining days – readying myself –
    for death, and the bright eternity of my Saviour's smile.

Paulet

Christian souls should spend all their days so.

Mary

You've taken away my serving men and my chambermaids.
    What has become of them?

Paulet

Good day, Madame.

Mary

Don't turn your back on me, sir!

Your silence is a torment! If you hope to terrify me you
    have succeeded.
I confess my fears: I fear not knowing – I fear a murderer's
    footstep
in the smothering darkness – I fear to die out of my
    Saviour's presence.
Imagined horrors were ever worse than bitter certainties.

Kennedy

Madame – he'll grant us nothing.

Mary

A month ago – less than a month –
I was shaken from my sleep, hurried and carried, unwarned,
    unprepared –
and set before Elizabeth's commissioners –
forty or more or them – shouting accusations – gross insults.
They crept out of the darkness of the night like ghosts –
baying and gibbering if I faltered – jeering when I whispered
    my innocence –
confusing me with unanswerable questions –
rushing me, stumbling into subtle argument – set about
    with traps and snares.
I had no time to think – look back – no advocate allowed
I had no friend to speak for me – nor knew my accusers,
    nor anything of their purposes.
Yet I sensed – no, I was certain! – it was not the *truth* of
    me they wanted.
They sought merely the form of the thing – the mockery
    of a trial – its false legality –
So they might say it had been done.
And then the show dissolved –
back into shadows like demons at cockcrow.

Who were those things of hate and spite? Were they my
    judges and jury?
What court was that – what painted show of justice – a
    comedy?
Since that night there's been no word –
in your face nothing to read – these glassy eyes, cold and
    comfortless.
I beg you, break your silence!
Tell me what your masters have resolved – Lord Burghley
    and the rest!
I hope – I *know* your Queen, Elizabeth, believes my innocence,
but will my innocence prove sufficient, weighed against
    Burghley's pitiless policy.
Say what may I hope for? Show me what I should fear?

Paulet (*after a pause*)

You must hope that God will be merciful.

Mary

I've never doubted God. Justice in England is less certain.

Paulet

O you'll have justice –

Mary

But when? What's been decided?

Paulet

I can't say –

Mary

Do you know?

Paulet

No. No – I'm told nothing –

Mary

There's no death warrant?

Paulet

I know nothing.

Mary

They'll come at night again – but not the commissioners.
Out of the darkness will creep my murderers.

Paulet

At each day's end we should place our souls in the hands
    of God.
No man can know when he will be called to judgement.
Better be ready then.

Mary

I know Lord Burghley seeks my life.
My deposition – and my death – are his life's work.
He'd corrupt any court, bribe any judge, to have me
    condemned.
But would Elizabeth – dare Elizabeth – sign the warrant,
then set her seal upon a lying instrument
while all Europe looks on? I will not think she dare.

Paulet

Her Majesty is no man's fool.
She listens only to God, to her conscience, and to Parliament.

Enter **Mortimer**.

Paulet

When your fate is decided she will act swiftly and fearlessly,
calling this world, and the world to come, to witness her
    justice

Mary

Her justice –

Mortimer (*ignoring* **Mary** – *it seems to be a studied insult*)
Uncle – they're here.

He exits.

Mary

Your own rudeness, Sir Amyas, I put down to lack of feeling
and the natural testiness of age,
but I will no longer suffer the insulting manner of your
    nephew –

Paulet

Edward Mortimer learned his manners in your own France,
    Madame.
If they displease you, blame the nation not the boy.
I couldn't change him if I wanted to, and nor will you,
    I know.
He could never abide a Catholic.

He exits.

Kennedy

Insulting man!

Mary

Sir Amyas is no flatterer. Why should he be?
What favours could his flattery win of me – desolate as I am?
Yet there's honesty beneath his harshness –
were I to search it out I might find some comfort – even a
    little sweetness there.

Kennedy

You're wrong, Lady.
I see they've quite destroyed your spirit.

Mary

They could never do that. But my own conscience might . . .
I'm sinking, sinking –

Kennedy

You've been my rock – my strong tower!
Now, in old age, I must be your nurse once more.
I've watched over you from a baby – often chided you for
  lightness, never till now for despair –

Mary

You know what day this is.

Kennedy

I do, I do. But, Lady, that was twenty years ago –

Mary

My wretched husband – poor unhappy boy –
cries from the beneath the granite slab we laid upon him.
I see his burnt and broken body –

Kennedy

No, My Lady –

Mary

blackened and bleeding –
His startled eyes stare through me – into the guilty places
  of my soul.

Kennedy

He cannot hurt you now –

Mary

He can. He does!
His spirit will not let me sleep – his blood calls out for mine.
This is the day they murdered him.

Kennedy

Your tears washed out the guilt – years of weeping – years
  of penitence –
Our Saviour and His Church absolved you –

Mary

I've not absolved myself.
How can I when I see his wounds bleed still?
Will nothing heal them? – no incense, tinkling bells,
nor altar boys skying their penitential psalms to heaven,
nor this little crucifix, nor the comfortable words of a
    confessor
can scrub away the horrors from my mind.
He's waiting, waiting – sensing my time has come –

Kennedy

You didn't murder Darnley –

Mary

While others slaughtered him I looked on. I did nothing –
    nothing! –

Kennedy

You were a child.

Mary

And so was he. I was no innocent.

Kennedy

He deserved his death.
He was a monster! – brainsick – vicious –
You raised him from nothing – he aimed at your throne
    and crown
and would have taken them by force.
He repaid your love with hatred – no one was safe from
    his lust –
Did he not butcher young David Rizzio before your eyes?
The life they took was lawful – a just revenge.

Mary

Revenge is never just – it's forbidden by our faith.
The comfort you intend merely opens new wounds.
O . . . he gave me this ivory box –

She picks up some of the pieces.

Kennedy

God will forgive you – or why else is He God?

Mary

Will He? I married the man who struck my husband down.

Kennedy

O it was a shameful thing! But still, God will forgive it.

Mary

I was Queen of Scotland at six days old – at sixteen years
    Queen of France –
my first two husbands were boys.
When I grew to a woman I wanted – I thought I needed –
    a man's protection.
Bothwell – the man – the protector I chose, murdered my
    boyish husband –
I lured Darnley to his death!

Kennedy

Shameful. God will forgive you.

Mary

Now they're coming to take my life.
How can I approach God's judgement seat –
hold out my hands to Him with a husband's blood upon
    them?
Go, Hannah, go! Beg them to send me a priest –

Enter **Mortimer**.

Mortimer

I must speak to the Queen – alone –

Kennedy

Don't roar at me, you puppy dog –

Mortimer

You've nothing to fear –

Mary

Don't leave me, Hannah –

Mortimer

Lady – this letter must speak for me.
Mistress Kennedy, stand at the door – warn us if you hear
    my uncle.

Mary
From France! The Cardinal's seal – my mother's brother –

Mortimer
Read it – quickly –

Mary
Hannah – do as he says. Wait outside the door.

She does.

'You have no truer friend than Edward Mortimer
who brings this letter. Trust him in all things.
Charles, Cardinal of Lorraine, your loving uncle.'

Mortimer
Now burn it. Burn it – I beg you, Madame.

Mary
What can I believe?
I'm sinking into despair – you'll raise me up only to cast
    me down –
lower, and lower – to break my spirit.
Young man, you have always treated me with such contempt,
why should I trust you now?

Mortimer
Forgive me!

He kneels and kisses her hand.

Royal Lady, forgive these times –
I'm forced to disguise my loyalty –
Trust me! – as my uncle Paulet trusts the mask of callousness
    I wear –
for by its means I've come to you with messages of hope! –
With news of friends who'll help you to escape –

Mary
No! No, I –

Mortimer
This is no time to doubt.
Your bitterest enemy is here –

But we'll defeat him! – with the help of heaven, and loving
   friends –

Mary

Who is my enemy? Where are my friends?

Mortimer

I am your friend.

Mary

This paper tells me so. This dangerous paper . . .
Who are you, sir?

Mortimer

A convert to your faith and to your cause.

My own religion – bludgeoned into me while still a child –
   grew from fear of Rome.
They said the Pope was anti-Christ, performing Satan's rites
   for all who'd sell their souls.
They schooled my childish innocence in the terrors of hell:
Every line is inked in black – every word written in hatred –
   every sentence to be feared;
Look only for retribution, look for punishment, fear loss of
   salvation.
And no word of their ranting and roaring may be questioned.
They showed me nothing of love! – nothing of love's power.
In my twentieth year – I thought to anneal my joyless faith
in the flames of hell itself – I went to Rome.
It was a time of festival – every wayside crucifix stood
   garlanded with flowers –
and upon each road – each crooked pathway – a stream –
a river of humanity flowed towards the eternal city –
pilgrims swept onward by joy – carrying me with them into
   those still, deep waters.
Rome – calm and sure!
It was as if the gates of Paradise, hinged with song,
swung open to receive my newborn soul into the world
   of light.
For all man's art – labouring a thousand years to praise his
   Creator's name –

rose up before me – wondrous illumination! The music of
the spheres!
I saw the cherubim and seraphim hovering about the throne
of God
I saw angels and archangels – thrones, dominions, powers –
I saw the Blessed Virgin, and Our Saviour's birth,
I saw Our Lord, transfigured, ascending to heaven . . .

And then the Mass . . . and heaven reaching out to me.
I watched this worthless world of kings and emperors sink
into clay.
I understood eternity. I looked upon the God's mystery –
and entered His world of love.

Mary
My heart will break for what I'll never see.
Your vision of true freedom serves only to darken my prison.

Mortimer
No prison could be dark that harbours you, Lady –
The treasure it hides shines brighter than Elizabeth's court –
It is a hallowed shrine of gold, and precious stones –

Mary
In England men destroy their shrines – the holy relics spill
into the rubble –

Mortimer
Lord Burghley is wise to keep you captive – hidden away –
For if that face were seen, all England's youth would mutiny,
shake swords in Elizabeth's face – rioting in the London
streets –

Mary
I've seen too many swords.

Mortimer
You're their rightful Queen! England's Queen!

Mary
That right has been my curse. That right will ruin me.

Mortimer
We have so little time –

Mary
Then tell me – quickly! – have my judges reached a verdict?

Mortimer
O Lady –

Mary
Tell me. No words can kill me.

Mortimer
Guilty. They found you guilty –
Forty-two commissioners, and the House of Lords – the
    Commons of England,
and the Citizens of London – pronounce you guilty . . .
Of plotting Elizabeth's assassination and of aiming at
    her throne.

Mary
And the sentence?

Mortimer
As yet, none.
They're asking for your death. But Elizabeth alone has
    power to sentence you.

Mary
What does she say?

Mortimer
Nothing. She holds back.

Mary
Then there's still hope –

Mortimer
She counterfeits clemency, while prompting the Privy Council
    to force her eager hand –
seeming to say: 'I would not sign – but, since you'll have
    it so, I must – '
O she'll sign – believe it! She's merciless – nature's withered
    up in her –
she's utterly heartless.

Mary

Poor woman – to be so misjudged!

Henry the Seventh was grandfather to us both. Elizabeth
will never shed the royal blood that runs in her own
veins. No. She'll keep me here in darkness – silence –
smothering justice – denying me my voice.

Mortimer

You're England's rightful heir!

Let go all hope of her. Can illegitimate Elizabeth possess
your throne in quiet?

While you're alive her fears live on.

Mary

She'll not execute a queen – twice crowned, and twice
anointed with the holy oil –

elected in heaven to wait on heaven's King and do his
bidding on earth.

The voices of angels will shout down those who speak
against me.

To strike at me is to strike at monarchy itself – she won't
do that.

She calls herself Queen – she dare not show her people the
way to kill a sister.

Mortimer

O you do not know her!

Mary

Elizabeth would not offend my brother the King of France –
she would not dare!

Mortimer

France and England kiss! They've signed a perpetual peace!

Elizabeth has agreed to give herself in marriage to the
Duke of Anjou –

The King of France will be *her* brother –

Mary

Dear God! Then Spain – King Philip of Spain –

Mortimer

England and France will laugh at Spain – they'll be
invincible, once joined together.

Mary

I cannot think the people of England –

Mortimer

My Lady, I beg you, place no faith at all in the people of
England.
The English are fickle – fickleness itself – blown like feathers
in the wind –
from Rome to Canterbury – and back to Rome – from Italy
to perdition.
For years they barred Elizabeth from the throne, but then
they made her Queen.
Your idle people cheered her mother's marriage to
Henry VIII,
but not so loudly as they jeered at her, howling her to
the block.
And Catherine Howard too – and Lady Grey – both queens,
crowned and anointed.
Scotland may be a savage nation, Lady, but the English
wash their hands in blood.
The mob gapes at a coronation, but is lashed to joyful
frenzy at an execution.

Mary

I have no fear of death, but only the manner of it.
I fear the assassin in the night
I fear to die in silence, denied the comforts of religion, my
cause unheard.

Mortimer

Royal Lady, you will not die.
There's twelve of us have taken the sacrament to set you free.
The French Ambassador, Count Aubespine, has planned
it all –

Mary

No! O poor, deluded boy!

She burns the letter he gave her.

> Young men have tried to rescue me before.
> Go see! – their heads grin down at you from London Bridge.
> Fly! You must fly! I've too much blood on my soul already.
> Lord Burghley knows your plans – be sure of it –
> his spies have every detail – more likely the plot's his own.
> One of your twelve will be a traitor, certainly –
> Have you not heard? There's one in every twelve.
> Go to Rome – or France –
> My uncle of Lorraine will help you –
> Mary's cause is lost! Save your lives!

Mortimer
> Royal Lady, no! I'm not afraid –

Mary
> I am! My only rescue's in Elizabeth –
> My only hope is that she'll be merciful –
> These plots of yours can only damage me.

Mortimer
> You're lost indeed! Elizabeth merciful? Then so's the devil!

Mary
> I am not lost!
> There is one man – and it's not you – who can persuade
>   her of my innocence.

Mortimer
> What man? What man could rescue you?

Mary
> O dare I speak his name?

Mortimer
> You must trust me, Lady! Your uncle, the Cardinal –

Kennedy
> Sir Amyas is coming –

Mortimer
> For the love of God! Trust –

Mary
I must! I must believe that God has sent you here
to be my angel-messenger – take him this letter –

Mortimer
Take who – ?

Mary
Leicester. The Earl of Leicester.

Takes a letter from her bosom.

Mortimer
No! He's your bitterest enemy – Elizabeth's minion.
When the Council called for your execution Leicester's
    voice was loudest –

Mary
Quickly! Deliver the letter – my salvation!
We've had no means to get it to him – I feared your uncle –

Kennedy
He's coming, he's coming – and there's someone with him.

Mortimer
Madness!

Mary
Leicester will welcome you. That letter is my life, go now!
    Go –
And thank you – thank you! And the love that brought you –

He kneels and kisses her hand. There's the sense that it's a little too much.

Mortimer
My Lady!

He exits.

Mary
May God go with you.

Enter **Burghley, Paulet** *and* **Drury**.

Burghley
Mary Stuart.

Mary
Lord Burghley. Will you sit?

He does so.

Paulet
Leave us, Mistress Kennedy.

Kennedy
Majesty?

Mary
Hannah, you have leave to go.

Paulet
This morning, Lady, you asked me if I knew the verdict
of your judges.
Lord Burghley himself has come to speak to you.

Burghley
Sit, Lady Stuart.

She does not.

I come from the Privy Council –

Mary
Not from my sister? Not from Elizabeth?

Burghley
No –

Mary
You are her Council's shepherd, sir.
The Council hears your voice and follows you. Bleating.
For all your sheepish looks, sir – don't be afraid to let me
know the worst.

Burghley
The worst? Then you are privy to the Council's decision?

Mary
I guess at it.
Lord Burghley would not ride to Fotheringhay
to make Queen Mary merry with the news of her release.

Or have I misjudged your malice to me?
You may speak.

Burghley

I have no malice, Lady – I make policy.
You submitted yourself to the verdict of forty-two judges –

Mary

Stop there. I did no such thing. I submitted myself, though
    most unwilling,
to the interrogation of my enemies. Nor would I – could I –
    have agreed
to proceedings so prejudicial to my majesty, to my person,
and to the kingly hopes of James, my son and heir.
Those creatures of the night were never a *court* – how could
    they be?
How could they pass judgement on a prince of the blood?
Let me remind you, Lord Burghley, of the laws of England:
Those laws set down that the accused shall be tried by a
    jury of his peers.
Who are my peers, sir? Though they did their work in
    darkness
I believe I saw no kings among my accusers. And anointed
    kings – or queens – are my only peers.

Burghley

Why then did you answer them?

Mary

Out of respect for my sister, Queen Elizabeth, whose
    messengers they were.
I never supposed them my equals, nor judged them judges,
    nor were they so.

Burghley

And yet they have judged you.

Mary

Every ploughman, dairymaid, and privy councillor judges
    me, sir!
But such vulgar comment has no force in English law.

Burghley

Lady Stuart, you came to England of your own free will.
You breathe our English air – you ask protection – England
comforts you. Say – are you not subject to our English
law?

Mary

The air I breathe is God's, sir, and as for England's comfort
and protection I've seen little enough of either in my prison
But certainly, though not England's subject, I will admit
I'm subject to English law. That law allows me judgement
by my peers.

I ask again, who are my equals?

Burghley

True, Lady, your judges were not your equals. There were
among them, or so I think, no murderers or adulterers,
nor any French poisoners like your mother's kin, nor
perpetrators of Paris massacres like your brothers-in-law,
nor papal lackeys like your uncle Guise, no cock-chick,
pox-ridden lechers like the boy Darnley – your chosen
second husband, with whom you, and his whores, female
and male, were one flesh – nor drink-sodden pirates like
Lord Bothwell, who blew up your husband's lodgings
with his powder kegs, to gain your easy love, and had it
too – before and after you were wed!   Your judges,
Lady, are this land's nobility! – impartial Englishmen –
men without equal.

No hint of scandal's ever 'smirched their names: among
them George Talbot, Earl of Shrewsbury; good John
Whitgift, Archbishop of Canterbury; and Howard of
Effingham, the Lord High Admiral; the Earl of Leicester
too! – Where could a better man be found to find your
faults? There *are* no better, nor more faithful men – and
you had forty-two of them. And forty of that forty-two
pronounced you guilty. Guilty, Lady!

Mary (*after a silence*)

The violence of your language silences me.

Yet were the nobility of England the honourable men you
    claim –
upright, impartial, wise – and free to judge according to
    their consciences –
how could I not, for shame, submit myself to them?
But are they such men? Do such men exist?
I remember that same nobility of England – some of them
    you've named –
In the days of my great-uncle Harry the Eighth skipping
    like eunuchs
in the harem of the Ottoman Turk to whatever tune their
    preposterous master
was pleased to call. I remember your House of Lords
scrambling to cancel each afternoon the laws they'd made
    in the morning.
I remember them running like rabbits to reverence His
    Holiness the Pope
when he named bloated Harry 'Defender of the Catholic
    Faith',
then, when it suited that faithless waverer to attack the faith
    he'd sworn ever to defend,
his pack of lords proclaimed His Holiness the anti-Christ!
I remember those same lords – forever scurrying, changing,
    legitimising, bastardising,
divorcing, marrying, recognising, disinheriting, promoting,
    disgracing, executing –
yes, executing – and all to please their feckless, fickle King.
As for their faith, Englishmen change it with their linen, sir,
four times in as many reigns. Such sinful faithfulness should
    cast no stone at me.

Burghley

We've lived through troubled times.

Mary

Then put an end to them!

Burghley

That's my intention – that's my policy.

Mary

My Lord, I believe you prize your loyalty to Elizabeth above
all things.

Love of your country, not hatred of me, drives you – as it
should – to great extremity.

Be open then! You have no need to curb nor spur the law.

Let truth and justice do their work unchecked.

Abandon secrecy, throw over subterfuge, contrive no plots,

bribe no false witnesses, be open to the public gaze, and
heaven's scrutiny.

And, be assured, I can prove my innocence. Let me speak
to my sister!

Question your conscience: can a Scottish queen ever have
justice from an English judge?

What Protestant's unprejudiced against a Catholic?

But question why it's so! Should not England and Scotland
be natural allies?

Yet down the centuries Scotland has comforted England's
enemies,

and down the centuries every civil war fought upon Scottish
soil has been

devised, promoted, armed, and sustained by the English
crown.

Believe me, sir, the hatred between our nations can never
turn to love

until one sceptre sways our lands as one – until two crowns
are set upon one head.

Burghley

You hoped a Stuart would hold sway – would wear those
crowns?

Mary

I did – I do. I confess I do – why should I deny it?

I long to see our stormy kingdoms shelter beneath a single
olive bough,

teaching each other the gentle arts of peace –

Burghley

And, to accomplish this, you'd kill Elizabeth and filch her
throne –

Unity through bloodshed, and inciting civil war –
You'd burn our new-fledged faith on instruction from Rome –

Mary

Never! Where is your evidence?

Burghley

Written. Your own hand condemns you –

Mary

I swear by God in heaven I am innocent of all plots.
Your assertions are no proofs – show me the letters – show
    me my hand in them!

Burghley

Babington and his conspirators were your instruments –

Mary

So you have said. Show me the documents.

Burghley

The documents were produced at your interrogation.

Mary

Copies! – written by your own secretaries – even your
    forty-two judges admitted that –

Burghley

Copied from your letters found on Babington –

Mary

Show me the originals!

Burghley

Babington confessed –

Mary

Under torture – to your own fictions –

Burghley

He confessed!

Mary

But not to me – not before me!
As God is my witness I wrote no letters –

and the world has only your word, Burghley, for Babington's
   confession.
Why was he put to death in such haste, My Lord?
Why was he not brought before the court?
Why was he not questioned before my face?

Burghley

Gilbert Kurl and Claude Nau, your own secretaries,
whom you've deemed honest men, confessed you dictated
   those letters –

Mary

They've confessed no such thing! Not before me.
What – have you bribed them? – Or did you torture them
   too?

Burghley

Lady Stuart –

Mary

How do I know they're still alive?

Burghley

Of course they're alive –

Mary

Then God be praised, and keep them living still!
Bring them before me – and let them repeat these lies
   before their Queen.
There is a law in England – is it not so? – accuser and
   accused must face each other?
Bring me my accusers – bring me Kurl and Nau.
Sir Amyas Paulet – you're an honest man – tell me the truth,
is this not English law?

Paulet

It is. I'll not deny it.

Mary

I demand justice! I demand the law of England!
You make your laws to oppress the innocent,
do not deny them when they seem to favour me.
Your law says Babington should have been set before my
   face.

Why was he not? My Lord, answer me!
No? Then where are my secretaries Kurl and Nau?
If they have evidence to place let them bring it before me.

Burghley

Calmly, Lady, calmly.
That you plotted with Babington is not the only charge
   against you –

Mary

It's the only capital charge –

Burghley

You've had secret communications with the Spanish
   Ambassador –

Mary

Oh! More fictions. Bring your proofs. Answer my questions:
Where are Kurl and Nau? Why wasn't Babington produced?
No more put-offs –

Burghley

I have proof that you have contemplated inciting
all the Catholic monarchies of Europe to come to your aid.

Mary

Contemplated! God in Heaven! Now he accuses me of
   contemplation!

Burghley

Lady –

Mary

Guilty! I plead guilty!
I have contemplated escape, I have contemplated growing
   wings and flying free,
I have contemplated English injustice, English barbarity –
of all this I am guilty! Guilty! Guilty! Will contemplation
   hang me?
Contemplate this, My Lord: I came to my sister queen a
   suppliant.
Hospitality is her sacred duty –
to a woman in distress, to a friendly power, and to her family.

Yet contrary to every law of every civilised nation, contrary
to her sex –
and contrary even to her misguided religion – she imprisoned
me.
What sisterly ties should bind me to her?
What ties of conscience should keep me prisoner in her
kingdom?
Like every little soul I want my freedom!
Freedom's the right of every innocent man and woman –
freedom, justice – and a right to plead my case according
to good laws.
But, as I've sworn – I'll swear again before you now –
I never have, nor never will, plot her overthrow nor call
for her murder.
I've a conscience, sir, that would never permit so deep
a stain upon my soul and honour.
I bear my sister no ill will. I believe that, if she knew me,
she'd bear me none neither.
O I'll have freedom by whatever lawful means I can –
by my own weak power if needs must –
but I'd far rather have it by Elizabeth's grace and favour.

Burghley

All power's gripped in her hands.

Mary

But not justice! She cannot strangle truth!
There is no law, of God nor Englishmen, to justify my
death –
not by public execution, nor by secret murder.
Heaven and the world look on.
Contemplate that, Lord Burghley.

She exits.

Burghley

You see how things are with her, Sir Amyas?
Leave us, Drury.

Exit **Drury**.

Burghley

Monstrous! Stubborn!

What's looser than the tongue of an unmanned woman!

She resists the law – juggles with truth! – O she'll never
    confess . . .

I swear that when her neck's upon the block – pray God
    it's soon! –

she will deny her guilt still – and proclaim her innocence –

glorying in treacherous thoughts of bogus martyrdom!

And there lies my difficulty, Sir Amyas – that's our difficulty.

London loves a burning but it loves a martyr more.

And the longer Elizabeth wavers and delays, the stronger
    grows Mary's following.

The world is softening – even her enemies begin to pity her.

Paulet

Presented with your proofs, she'd not defy us.

Babington should have been made to confront her in open
    court –

Now she must face her secretaries, Kurl and Nau –

Burghley

She must not! Never.

If Kurl is forced to face her he'll retract. If Kurl breaks
    down the other's word is void.

We cannot allow her to question them – her first tear would
    weaken Kurl's resolve –

at the sight of her distress all would be lost.

Paulet

O, if only she'd never crossed our border – stayed in Scotland!

Burghley

True – the Scots are accomplished cut-throats – they've
    no use for pity there –

Or better she'd stayed widowed in her France.

Paulet

Amen to that! I blame that day I ever set eyes upon her.

Burghley

A gentler, more considerate lady
would have soon despaired of her imprisonment, taken ill
and died.

Paulet

I think she lives still merely to spite us all.

Burghley

Yet if she died they'd blame us for her death.

Paulet

The worser sort will always think the worst.

Burghley

There'd be no proof, of course. Rumour's a harmless storm.

Paulet

Rumour never sank a ship. Proven guilt's what hangs a man.

Burghley

Or woman.

Sir, you may be wrong.
I've often noted that strong opinion – a fixed prejudice –
holds mastery over justice weakly grasped.
But then opinion often bares its teeth at rigour –
pities the condemned, and blames the judge for harshness.
I know Elizabeth.
Vain – feminine – she prizes the mob's applause.
She values a show of mercy above all other attributes of
royalty –
I say 'a show' of mercy.
Were the world not looking on she'd wield a sword, or swing
an axe
with more relish than her dreadful father –
whom Jesu pardon –

Paulet

Whose soul God rest –

Burghley

But to let all-seeing Christendom pry while she cuts off the
head of another woman –

a queen – her cousin?
It's a course too bloody – too terrible to imagine!
I know Elizabeth – I fear she'll never sign the death warrant.
She'll falter – put off – do nothing –
and at the last she'll exercise her royal prerogative –
grant Mary a pardon.

Paulet

And if she does –

Burghley

No, no – she cannot – it's not to be thought upon!
While Mary lives weeds of conspiracy root, and tangle
around her.
The Pope has published a bull, calling for Elizabeth's
assassination.
I see daggers behind every bush – every Arras cloth –
poison in every cup.
Some part of my every waking hour is wasted on this
problem.
As for the Queen herself – no sleep for her! Each night's
disturbed with terrors –
nightmares of her assassination, or horrors at the thought
of Mary's public execution –
Impossible choice! Impenetrable equation! On the one
hand to be the mark
that every murderer stabs or shoots at; on the other, to be
herself an executioner
with a tarnished crown – fallen from grace – deprived of
her people's love and warmth.

Paulet

There is no other choice. It must be one or the other –
hers the decision.
She is the Queen. Her hand is guided by heaven.

Burghley

There is another way: if other hands were guided by loyalty
and duty.

Paulet

Duty?

Burghley

You've been set to watch a poisonous spider, Sir Amyas –
you protect that bottle of venom as if it were a precious
     jewel.

Paulet

The most precious jewel I know is Queen Elizabeth's
     reputation.
I'll protect that with my life.

Burghley

Let me be blunt. And be sure I speak with Queen Elizabeth's
     voice:
When Mary Stuart was removed from the keeping of the
     Earl of Shrewsbury,
and given into yours, it was hoped –

Paulet

That I would undertake this most odious of commissions
     faithfully, and honourably.
I hope that's what you were about to say. My reputation
     has no stain upon it, My Lord.
My loyalty and my duty have never been called in question –

Burghley

Your reputation would remain spotless.
Let rumour of a wasting sickness prepare the world for
     Mary's death.
Her death will follow when the world's expecting it.
All memory of her will soon wither and die –

Paulet

And with it would wither and die my conscience.

Burghley

Surely, Sir Amyas, you could not suppose that I was asking
     you to – ?

Paulet

I did suppose it.

Burghley

Then you were wrong. We'd find some subtle stranger who –

Paulet

Will never come under my roof.

I'll have none of your assassins in my house – no poisoners,
    nor torturers of the mind.

To me a prisoner's life's as sacred as my sovereign's.

You hold the law in your hands, My Lord – Jesu! is that not
    enough?

If she's conspired against the Queen then give her justice!
    Justice!

Judge her, condemn her, behead her –

I'll welcome the carpenter that comes to build her scaffold –

the sheriff who brings me her death warrant,

and the headsman who brings the axe.

But I'll shut my door against all others.

I know my duty, sir.

She'll do no evil while she's in my care,

and no evil – none – will ever be done to her.

Act Two

Music. A most impressive masque. The Castle of Beauteous Chastity is besieged by the Forces of Desire. A champion (the **Earl of Leicester** *in the persona of Faithful Duty) protects the castle from assaults by Lust. Lust is defeated. Then* **True-Love's Champion** *(a French lord) comes into the lists. The castle is bombarded by cannon shots of perfume and flowers.* **True-Love's Champion** *overthrows Faithful Duty.*

True-Love's Champion *(singing)*
> *Nostra sventura è ben che qui s'impieghi*
> *tanto valor dove'l silenzio il copra.*
> *Ma poi che sorte ria vien che ci neghi*
> *e lode e testimoni degni de l'opera,*
> *pregoti, se fra l'arme han loco i prieghi,*
> *che 'l tuo nome e 'l tuo stato a me tu scopra,*
> *acciò ch'io sappia, o vinto o vincitore,*
> *chi la mia morte o la mia vita honore.*

The castle opens.

Chastity *(singing from above)*
> *Castità! Purezze!*

Chastity *descends from the tower, and lifts up* **True-Love's Champion***, presenting him with a ring. Then* **Chastity** *ascends to heaven, leaving* **True-Love's Champion** *perplexed.*

Davison
> And Chastity flies off to heaven. That won't please the French.

Kent
> Painted fabric and paper crowns. In real life Chastity's about to surrender her castle.

Davison
> I wouldn't be so sure. Elizabeth won't marry a Frenchman.

Kent

She'll marry the French King's brother – the contract's
   signed and sealed.
The Duke of Anjou –

Davison

Agreed – not yet signed and sealed. Anjou's a Catholic –

Kent

He's to be allowed Mass in his private chapel, on condition
   he swears
to recognise, honour, and defend the Church of England
   and the Protestant Succession.
And he's agreed! Every obstacle's removed – Elizabeth will
   give her people an heir –

Davison

If it pleases God –

Kent

If it pleases God the Stuart claim is dead and buried.
Mary's no longer a threat – if France abandons her –

Davison

The Pope –

Kent

The Pope! Let the Pope and Philip of Spain marry each
   other.

Enter **Queen Elizabeth** *at her most magnificent, on the arm of the*
Earl of Leicester, *still dressed as Faithful Duty, with* **Aubespine**
the French Ambassador, **Bellievre**, *a French lord, emissary from the*
Duke of Anjou, **Talbot***, the* **Earl of Shrewsbury**, *and other*
French and English gentlemen.

Elizabeth

My Lord Ambassador – Count Aubespine, I am desolate.
Our homely entertainment shames us – and our Court.
O sir, forgive our kindly meant simplicity.
The young gentlemen of France, we hear, have grown
   accustomed to a magnificence,

in their festivals, and holy days, unimaginable in this my
poor isle.
They say the mother of your King, Catherine de Medici,
who brought such splendour –
all the riotous extravagance of her native Italy – to the
Court of St Germain,
spends more on banquets, palaces, and finery than we do
on our fleet.
I can scare afford to give a beggar charity.
And yet they love me – my people love me.
What shows and pageants, what tournaments and revelry
can equal
the joyous outpouring of good hearts? I feel it every time
I go among them:
they rush upon me in their thousands – thronging to gaze
and cheer –
shouting their vulgar blessings as if I were some wonder . . .
not merely their guardian and careful queen.
I have, and hear a Nation's love. That's more to me than
majesty and show.

Aubespine

You are a wonder, Royal Lady – the wonder of your sex.

Elizabeth

The burden I bear would tax the strength of men and yet
I bear it –
that is the only wonder.

Bellievre

Highest Majesty, my royal master, Francis of Anjou,
begs you upon his knees to name your wedding day.

Aubespine

Royal Lady, now that all impediments and hindrances are
thrown down
it were good to set the time –

Bellievre

My Lord is young – quite overcome with love for you.

Elizabeth

Youth must learn patience then, Lord Bellievre.

My kingdom's sun is gone behind the clouds – clouds that
threaten terrors.

While so many of my misled subjects are dragged to
execution I must weep –

and think still of graves – not of strewing my bed with
bridal herbs and flowers.

Treason aims at my heart. Who knows when the blow
may fall?

Bellievre

Your heart will be safe in my young lord's love.

The might of France will shelter you from harm.

Elizabeth

I believe you, sir.

There was a time – when first I weighed the weight of
England's crown –

I thought I should serve my God, whose regent on earth
I am, with the devotion of a nun.

Everything of me would be given to the care of His people.

And, when Time called me back to Him,

the honourable words they'd carve and gild upon my tomb
would be:

'Here lies the virgin queen.' Could any monarch wish for
better fame?

But, like a nun, I've learned obedience: my heart is not
my own.

I know my people – fearful of that time when I am laid
in earth –

demand of me a greater sacrifice. And I must grant it them.

Though I have ruled with the strength of many men,

and – I have a right to claim it – the measureless authority
of a mighty king,

it is in my womanhood my power is greatest:

it is in my womanhood I may marry England to France;

it is in my womanhood I may give my people the heir they
long for –

and ensure for my kingdom a lasting peace.

God's laws – the natural law – must be obeyed:
If it is my people's wish, England's royal mistress shall take
  a master.

She is unable to resist glancing at **Leicester**.

Elizabeth
Unless I rebel against myself.
I confess, sometimes, I still harbour treacherous thoughts
  and doubts.
Why should womanhood – the better half of human kind –
  be subject to the other?

Polite, mild laughter from the English, mild confusion from the French.

Aubespine
Royal Lady, most noble vessel of every precious virtue,
Europe acknowledges no man on earth worthy to be your
  lord and master.
And yet –

Elizabeth
And yet?

Aubespine
And yet the part of you that's woman must be boarded,
  manned, and thrown down
if England's to have more princes of the Tudor blood –
  this you have accepted.
The brother of our King is handsome, young, and bold –

Elizabeth
Yes, sir, and he's my choice – have I not promised?
'*Che sera, sera,*' – what must be, cannot be . . . put off
  forever.
There's hardly a gentleman of Europe to whom I'd give
  myself with less unwillingness.
Tell him so – adding what flattering courtliness you will.

Bellievre
My Lord the Duke requests that you set down the wedding
  day.
If you delay, Highest Majesty –

Elizabeth
What more can he demand? We live in uncertain times –
and while my kingdom's under siege from Rome –
Here, give him this token of my love – not yet a wedding
   ring:
let him think of it as the first link in the chain of iron and
   gold
that must fetter him. And –
Leicester. Kneel –

She removes his Order of the Garter ribbon from **Leicester***'s neck.*

Give him this too: *Honi soit qui mal y pense.*
Now let the ancient enmity, that too long divided our
   kingdoms,
dissolve into love, understanding, and perpetual peace.

Bellievre *kneels and receives the order.*

Bellievre
I receive this gift of love in the name of the Duke, my
   master,
and in his name swear faithfulness and homage.

Aubespine
Great Queen, when this is known
the bells of every steeple in England and France will peal
   out our peoples' joy,
and not be silenced till your wedding day is come.
Now is the time for mercy – sorrow itself must be imprisoned
and prisoned joy set free –

Elizabeth
Stop there, Ambassador. I see where you'd lead me –

Aubespine
Royal Lady –

Elizabeth
And I'll not be led there. Mary Stuart claims England's
   crown –
my nation – with whom yours must swear alliance. My
   enemies now are yours.

This woman has incited treason in my subjects and plotted
    my death.

Aubespine
    If that is proved –

Elizabeth
    It is proved. Forty judges have condemned her.

Aubespine
    My silence in this matter would dishonour me and expose
        France
    to accusations of neglect.
    Mary was once France's Queen. Humanity requires –

Elizabeth
    Your humanity, Ambassador, is noted.
    Do not meddle in matters that concern the safety of my
        realm –
    matters pertinent to me alone. You have leave.

The French bow out.

    Fetch Burghley.

Enter **Burghley**, *who kneels and kisses her hand, with* **Amyas**,
Paulet *and* **Mortimer**.

Elizabeth
    Sir Amyas, you may stay.
    Wait outside, young man.

Burghley
    Majesty, with this alliance England may find time to
        breathe –
    some respite from the pursuit of treasons that chase about
        your realm.
    But the greatest obstacle to our security remains.
    Your people cry to you – one final sacrifice they beg –

Elizabeth
    What now?

Burghley
    The head of Mary Stuart.

Elizabeth
No –

Burghley
For till it's off, your own will never lie in peaceful slumber –
    however soft the pillow –
untroubled by doubts and fears.
And nor will mine.
Mary is the hope, the head and fountainhead of all the
    devilish idolatry
that flows over your lands like a pestilence.
Catholic assassins, young men – who knows how many? –
    hundreds? – thousands? – move freely – unsuspected –
    through this kingdom, carrying within them her disease.
How may we know them? They have no hidden blemishes –
    no witches' marks –
to give away their murderous confederacy.
Stand one man, picked from a crowd, against another and
    tell me who's the traitor,
who's the honest man?
How can we know them till they strike? – and then's too late.
But strike they will – of that we may be sure. How? How
    may we be sure?
Because the Pope – the anti-Christ – proclaims that Mary's
    England's rightful Queen;
They're all young men – all sick with love for her – or
    rather the idol they imagine her.
To kill in her behalf's to do God's work – or so they're told
    – even to strike and fail
will earn them their reward – the name of martyr – and
    a throne in Roman heaven.
Majesty, our greatest danger lies in their certainty – the
    surety of their misbelief.
Our safety lies only in their unity for they have but one,
    single, fanatical aim –
to set the Stuart traitor on your throne.
Then, if she were gone, so were our fears. Cut off her
    head, the body of conspiracy dies. You are freed of all
    terrors.

Elizabeth
No man has greater care of me than Lord Burghley.
Can no one find me out a course less bloody? Lord
Shrewsbury?

Shrewsbury
Majesty, this land has never known such glorious days since
first God gave us kings.
I would not see your glory dimmed by an act offensive
to heaven.

Elizabeth
God forbid!

Shrewsbury
God has forbidden Mary's execution.
She is a twice-anointed queen − nor is she your subject.
You have no jurisdiction −

Elizabeth
My Lord. The Privy Council, the House of Lords, the City
of London −
every court and council in the land − with a single voice
say I am backed by law.
Can these good men − can all of them be wrong? Justice
herself condemns Mary −
it is no act of mine −

Shrewsbury
Why do you hesitate then?
Your counsellors and courts − England itself − are not the
theatre of the world.
The House of Lords is not the Court of Heaven.
Men are easily led − often swayed in judgement by a single,
plausible voice.
And one voice − though persuasive − may be false.

Burghley
Lord Shrewsbury −

Shrewsbury
We'd live in the age of gold if the advice that councils give
were never wrong.

But there never was a golden age –
when we look back it's ever wars, conspiracy, and overthrows.
If your heart inclines to mercy, Majesty, follow your heart –
then see with what urgency those who condemn her now
will swallow their advice and praise your clemency.
You must decide – you and you alone. What is majesty if
    it is not seen?
Monarchs may not hide behind such screens as Justice,
    Necessity, their councils, nor their people's will. *You* must
    sentence her.
And, as you judge, your people and the heavens will, in
    turn, judge you.
I tell you, trust your heart. Be merciful.

Elizabeth
Good old man, why do you favour my enemies?

Shrewsbury
Majesty, there's no one to speak for her but me. To raise
    an argument in her defence
is to invite your strong displeasure. How then may you
    come by the truth?
Yes, I am old. I'll soon be in my grave – that being so why
    should I flatter you?
I have no use for favour, no hopes of worldly gain, which
    makes the service I offer you – I mean the truth I tell –
    an object of great worth. Truth in your Court's become
    a rare commodity – all the more precious in times of
    great scarcity –

Burghley
My Lord –

Shrewsbury
Don't interrupt me. I do not judge her. How can I know
    if she's innocent or guilty?
The evidence against her – what I've seen of it – is highly
    suspect,
and, since she's allowed no advocate, I've heard nothing
    in her defence.

The Scots say she colluded in Lord Darnley's murder, and
  it's true,
she married her husband's murderer. Yes, she was weak –
  women are weak –

Elizabeth

Women are not weak. Some are stronger than the strongest
  men.

Shrewsbury

Your own childhood, Majesty, was instructed by experience
  and adversity,
hers by softness, idleness, and luxury. She was never equal
  to her task –

Elizabeth

Leicester. Have you anything to say?

Leicester

Did we come to gossip?
Are we members of the Privy Council? I can hardly
  believe it.
Who is Mary Stuart? A Frenchwoman that couldn't hold
  on to so poor a thing as the throne of Scotland.
How can she have serious hopes of yours?
She's in prison! Leave her there and forget her. Why stir
  up trouble?
What's the next business?

Burghley

Well here's a change! You voted for her death!

Leicester

That was in public. Things we must say in Parliament
  are often retracted in private –
as well you know, Lord Burghley. Her only hope was France.
Now that we've locked France in alliance, and masculine
  Elizabeth is to be brother to France's female king –

Elizabeth *smiles.*

Leicester

Mary's last hope must die –
her cause is fast expiring. You ask my advice, Madame?
    I say sentence her to death
but stay the execution. Let despair and frustration smother
    her in prison.
I can't think she'll live long. Any other business?

Elizabeth

My Lords, I thank you for your honest counsel, and your
    care of me.
Sir Amyas Paulet, who was that young man?

Paulet

My nephew, Majesty.

Elizabeth

Edward Mortimer? We remember him. Call him in.

Paulet

He has been travelling in Rome and France –

Elizabeth

We know.

Enter **Paulet**.

Paulet

I humbly beg you, Majesty, accept him into your service.

Mortimer

Royal Majesty.

He kneels.

Elizabeth

Welcome to Court, young Mortimer. How are my enemies
    in Reims and Rome? Thriving?

Mortimer

Confusion on them, Majesty!

Elizabeth

Whom did you meet there – Morgan? – that wicked Bishop
    Ross?

Mortimer
> I met them all – all the rebel Scotsmen – and crept into
> their confidence.

Elizabeth
> What are they plotting?

Mortimer
> The news that you are to ally yourself with France
> astonished them.
> They are thrown into amazement and despair. Now
> they pin their hopes on Spain.

Elizabeth
> So we hear.

Mortimer
> The Pope has reissued his bull excommunicating and
> deposing you.
> It was circulating in Reims when I was there.

Leicester
> That bull's grown old and feeble – he's lost his horns.

Elizabeth
> We hear also you renounced your Protestant faith in Reims.

She is studying him; tension.

> And that Charles of Guise, the Cardinal Archbishop, made
> you a Catholic.

She gasps.

Mortimer
> Yes, Majesty, I renounced my faith and swore myself to
> Rome and Mary's cause.

Paulet
> Here are letters, written in cipher by the Cardinal and his
> people, to Mary.
> My nephew handed them to me.

Burghley
> Good boy. I'll take them.

Elizabeth
And what's that other one?

Paulet
A letter to you, Majesty, written by my prisoner –

Burghley
I'll have that too –

He snatches at it.

Paulet
You'll pardon me, My Lord.

He hands it to **Elizabeth**. *She goes upstage and reads it.* **Mortimer**
whispers something to **Leicester** *which seems to alarm him.*

Burghley
Why should you trouble the Queen? It may contain

Paulet
I've seen the contents. She requests a meeting –

Burghley
Never!

Paulet
What harm can it do?

Burghley
Never!
The Queen cannot deal with murderers –
cannot negotiate with one who has sworn her death.

Paulet
The Queen may wish to be merciful. Who dare oppose
her wishes?

Burghley
I dare! Don't meddle, sir!
Mary's condemned to death – her head's on the block –
the axe must fall!
I know Her Majesty – if Mary pleads with her, her heart
will soften.

Elizabeth (*very moved – drying tears from her eyes*)
Kingdoms are clay, and life outlives the fleeting joys of youth.
We must be merciful, as we hope for mercy.
I too have pined in prisons – know what it is to live in fear
    of death.
How far she has fallen! – once Queen of France, and
    Scotland,
and once so sure of England's crown that England's arms
    were graven on her plate.
Pardon me, Lords. I must weep for her.

Shrewsbury
Royal Lady, obey the impulse of your heart –

Burghley
A rabid bitch should be destroyed.
Believe me, she still has teeth!

Elizabeth
Leave me!

They bow out.

(*To* **Mortimer**.) Young man. A word with you.

She looks him up and down with great deliberation.

The outward show is very fair. What's underneath?
So false so young, so practised in deception, and what
    ambition! I sense it – I feel it.
I can further it.

Mortimer
Majesty, I desire only to serve you –

Elizabeth
You've been in Rome. You know how unwavering my
    enemies are.
My crown's not safe while she's living.

Mortimer
Then cut her head off.

Elizabeth
If only that were the end of it!

If only the law were its own judge and executioner!
But no – first I must sign the warrant.
The thought of her blood on my hands – it's my own
    blood – so much blood terrifies me.
I turn to stone. This hand won't move.

Mortimer

Justice demands her death. Who dare condemn you?

Elizabeth

O there would be so many! – not openly – but I'd be hated
    for it.
Hated so deeply. And I want my people to love me.
It must be done secretly. Silently.
She must lie down in darkness – darkness must smother
    her – and when dawn breaks – when daylight steals
      through the morning mist into her chamber – she's gone.
That's how I'd have it done.

This hand of yours . . .

Mortimer

Majesty . . . Only say the word –

Elizabeth

No words.
We need no words – your thoughts speak to me with angel
    eloquence.
It's a task requiring all the passion of the young –
O this hand!

Mortimer

My hand is yours –

Elizabeth

Don't even whisper 'It is done!' Never tell me how or when.

Mortimer

Before the month is out –

Elizabeth

No more! Tell me no more. Think of your reward.
And don't take it ill if, publicly, I seem hardly to know you.

Those whom we love most are those whose love we most
deeply hide.

She gives him her hand to kiss and exits.

Mortimer
Bad. Bad. Clearly I look like a murderer.

Re-enter **Paulet**.

Mortimer
Is it something in my appearance? Something in my
manner? –

Paulet
What did she say to you?

Mortimer
Nothing – nothing, sir.

Paulet
You tread a dangerous path, young man. Beware of
ambition –

Mortimer
I am ambitious, sir – and I thought you ambitious for me.
You brought me here to Court –

Paulet
And now I begin to regret it. Don't endanger your soul!

Mortimer
I don't understand you –

Paulet
You do, you do! The Queen will promise you anything
but once you've served her purposes she'll destroy you –

Mortimer
Why should she?

Paulet
To keep her name! To guard her reputation.

Mortimer
'Served her purposes' – How? I don't know what you mean.

Paulet

Don't play the innocent with me, boy! I know what she's
asked of you.

Have you agreed to it? What have you undertaken –

Mortimer

Uncle –

Paulet

For, if you have, you can keep away from me, sir, and my
house

I'll have nothing more to do with you.

Enter **Leicester**.

Leicester

Gentlemen?

I'd speak with your nephew, Sir Amyas.

It is Her Majesty's pleasure you allow him access to the
Stuart woman whenever he wishes it.

Her Majesty expects great things of him.

Paulet

O does she!

Leicester

Yes, Paulet, she does.

Paulet

Good!

Leicester

Good?

Paulet

I know my duty, sir. Be sure I will perform it.

Leicester

Has anyone suggested anything to the contrary?

Exit **Paulet**.

Mortimer

My Lord, it's just an old man's jealousy. Her Majesty has
placed great trust in me.

Leicester
> Let's hope her trust is not misplaced.

He studies **Mortimer**.

Leicester
> You wished to speak to me. First, let me ask how can I be
>> sure of you?
> You possess two faces – one's worn for Elizabeth the other
>> for Mary Stuart.
> Which Queen sees the true face of Edward Mortimer –
>> Elizabeth, Mary, or neither?

Mortimer
> My Lord, you've nothing to fear –
> standing so high – nobody is closer to Her Majesty than
>> Leicester.
> I am nothing. Your frown would destroy me.

Leicester
> Keep that in mind . . . So how may we trust each other?

Mortimer
> I have a letter for you from the Queen –

Leicester
> The –

Mortimer
> Queen Mary –

Leicester
> God in heaven! If you speak of her, speak softly, man.

He quickly takes the letter, takes a portrait, a miniature from it, reads the
letter, weeps, seems to collapse physically, kisses the portrait.

Mortimer
> My Lord . . . I confess, I doubted when she spoke of you –
>> but these tears . . .
> I see her trust was not misplaced. Who could ask more
>> eloquent proofs?

Leicester
> You know what the letter says?

Mortimer

I know nothing. She says you're her last hope –

Leicester

Embrace me.

It's enough you've earned her trust. I may do nothing openly.

Because I stand so high, Burghley, Walsingham and the
    rest would give, each of them,

an eye to topple me. And they may do it yet.

After poor Mary I am the mark their hatred shoots at.

Mortimer

But I wonder, sir –

What draws you back so suddenly to Mary's side?

Leicester

I've never left it.

I've opposed her in the Parliament – swum with tides that
    flowed against her –

only that, privately, I may work for her good.

You know, I was once marked down to be her husband?

There was a time when the glories of heaven shone down
    upon her –

a life composed of warmth, of light, and laughter – a life
    I could have shared.

But I was proud. I drew back. I thought myself too bright
    a star

for Scotland's Queen to wear – I grew hard – flew too high!

Vanity, ambition, greed – a patchwork of cruel follies . . .

Now that my life's turned cold – now that she's sunk so low,

I'd lay down life and soul for her.

Mortimer

Could there be a more glorious act? – to die for her!

He's very slightly unhinged.

Leicester

Ambition was my downfall.

Elizabeth tempted me – seeming to offer herself – seeming
    to offer crowns.

It's a game she played – still plays – and with increasing
skill –

Mortimer

But . . . she's in love with you! The world thinks –

Leicester

Elizabeth loves to be loved.
I wooed her ten long years – my vanity puffing up hers –
enduring both her insults,
and her endearments . . . this most changeable of mistresses.
Now I am toyed with, fondled, smothered with kindness;
now I'm pouted at, trampled, flung aside – suffering
alternately the miseries of favour and disgrace.
But never, never, never may I stray out of her sight – out
of her reach.
And when I try – I do try – I'm browbeaten like a schoolboy,
raged at like some clumsy groom of her chamber . . .

Short pause.

If she were capable of being one thing for two hours
together
that thing would be Inconstancy itself.
Yet all her courtiers envy me my chains.

Mortimer

I pity you.

Leicester

Soon the brother of the King of France will push me from
my place.
Elizabeth's a woman – they say he's seventeen.
I thank my God for him – I pray they fetch him soon –
and leave me to look back on happier times.
There, in my memories, Mary's still enshrined in all her
brightness –
still rising in the morning of my hopes . . .
Her picture (*showing him*) shows me what I left behind –
when I adventured all I had on brittle, false Elizabeth.
If Mary can forgive me . . .

Mortimer
> You're a dreamer. Afraid of action –
> I see you'll do nothing for her – nothing!
> You voted for her execution –

Leicester
> I've told you why –

Mortimer
> Yes – 'policy'!
> I see it now – God chooses me alone to rescue her – to be
>   her saviour!
> You'd dream your life away – and hers!
> Without me you'd never even have received her letter.
> For all your influence – your fame – the task falls to me –

Leicester
> What are you saying? – what have you done? Are you –

Mortimer
> I have the means to rescue her –

Leicester
> No –

Mortimer
> By force! I came here hoping for your support.

Leicester
> Dear God! Have you spoken my name? Told –

Mortimer
> No! Coward!
> Nor would I now. Were it not for her misplaced faith in
>   you I'd not be here –

Leicester
> Force is the way to failure! It's what Burghley wants – what
>   he expects –
> just what he's waiting for –

Mortimer
> In twenty years, My Lord – twenty years! – you've
>   accomplished nothing.

Now, when heaven itself provides the means for her escape,
  you're supine –
Full of tears, and words –

Leicester
No power on earth can rescue her except Elizabeth's –

Mortimer
The power of God lies in this hand – this arm!

Leicester
Are you quite mad? You'll put her life in danger –

Mortimer
Her life *is* in danger – thanks to your delays –

Leicester
Folly! Madness! You're possessed –

Mortimer
Possessed by the Holy Spirit –

Leicester
God! You'll destroy everything I've worked for – years
  of subtle argument –
whispering in her ear: 'To destroy Mary is to kill all love
  for Elizabeth.'
If you corner her – if Elizabeth feels threatened – she'll
  strike out!
You think I've done nothing? I've kept Mary alive for
  twenty years –

Mortimer
Alive? Is that a life? – wasting away in prison – waiting
  for the blow to fall?
I'll tell you how much your words weigh with Elizabeth:
she's chosen me to murder Our Lady.

Leicester
She'd never sink so low – No!

Mortimer
She would – she has! She's tried to force my uncle to do it,
  and failed.

Why should I lie? But she's as deceived in me, as Mary is
    in you.

Leicester
How did you answer her?

Mortimer
I agreed to do it – willingly.
You said yourself Elizabeth expects great things of me –
now you know what those things are.
And, while she waits for me to act, Mary is safe from other
    hired assassins.

Leicester
God, God, God! . . . Well, it may buy us time –

Mortimer
Time? You've had twenty years! I've no more time to waste.

He starts to leave.

Leicester
Wait, Mortimer. Listen – think long and hard – open
    yourself to reason –
and calmly, calmly! Hear what I have to say.
I don't know what plots you've laid – nor do I wish to know.
But, of this be sure – be certain: Burghley's ahead of you.
Now he's so close to home – so close to Mary's execution –
d'you think he'd risk letting her escape?
How many times has a rescue been tried?

Mortimer
I've –

Leicester
And every time they fail!
Your uncle's no fool – watchful, suspicious –
your plotting with the Queen will make him doubly cautious.
Consider this: Burghley's deepest fear is that the two
    Queens should meet –
and I believe he's right to fear it. Consider why.
While Mary exists in Elizabeth's mind only as a threat – an
    idea – her life is in danger.

But if Mary became a face – a voice –
the very sweetness of her nature would disarm Elizabeth's
   fears.
If they once meet she'll never sign the order. I believe
   I can contrive that meeting.

Mortimer

No. What good would it do? She'd still be rotting in prison.
If you want to assist me, raise an army – capture Elizabeth –
hold her hostage in one of your castles – declare your love
   for Mary –
be her champion – prove yourself brave as Norfolk –
   Parry – me – or Babington!

Leicester

The three you name are dead. And you will follow them.
Your madness terrifies me, Mortimer – you'll be our
   destruction –

Mortimer (*going*)

Have you anything you wish me to say to her?

Leicester

Assure her of my constant love. Say I will do all I can –

Mortimer

Tell her that yourself. I'm not your pander – I'm her
   salvation.

He exits. **Leicester** *throws the letter on the fire, studies then pockets the picture.*

Enter **Elizabeth**.

Elizabeth

They heard raised voices. With whom were you arguing?

Leicester

Nobody of consequence. Your latest toy – your plaything.

Elizabeth

Young Edward Mortimer? Jealous?

Leicester

I hope you can trust him. Let me pass.

Elizabeth

What's wrong with –

Leicester

Your beauty is dazzling me. Let me go and obscure myself –
since I'm losing everything –

Elizabeth

What? What are you losing? Robin?

Leicester

I'm losing you to the Duke of Anjou –
Your adolescent champion, afire with love, royally hot-
blooded.
Madame, I'm no longer seventeen – my blood's not royal –
O you know the rest –

Elizabeth

Robin –

Leicester

Were I king, and you a serving maid, I'd raise you up –
this high.

He indicates her crown.

You lift me up only to throw me down – humiliating me
in front of the French! –
trusting Burghley's voice above my own!
Let me pass, Madame! Jesu! Marry a Prince of Frogs!

Elizabeth

Pity me then! I've not deserved your harshness.
My heart is not my own – you know it! I have proved my
love for you – how often!
How many more proofs must you have, Robin?

Leicester

I can never have proofs sufficient. You twist, and turn, and
change –
I've given everything! –

Elizabeth

You can't give me France!

She wishes she hadn't said it.

Leicester
> Were the world mine to give – and the next world too –
> they would be yours.

Uncomfortable pause.

Elizabeth
> I am the envy of all women. All women that are only
> women I envy.
> I am the fool of Fortune. The thing I'd give you – and most
> willing – the crown of England myself within it –
> I cannot – cannot do it. Crowns are the gifts of God –
> and heavy burdens. God forced this weight upon me –
> He'll not let me set it down.
> The Queen of Scotland put herself above her people –
> neglected her high calling –
> gave herself over to every pleasure – every vice – followed
> her heart –
> and men flocked to her – weak, vain men – old, young –
> all were destroyed at her fall –
> but still more come – like flies buzzing to rotting carrion.
> I will not fail as she failed.
> Nor will I not fail in love to you. Let's think no more of
> Mary Stuart.

She thinks about **Mary Stuart**.

Elizabeth
> I believe even old Lord Shrewsbury
> imagines himself young for her.

Leicester
> She bewitched him when she was his prisoner.

Elizabeth
> Her beauty's witchcraft then? Not painted on?
> It angers me to hear her praised so often – is she so regal?
> Is she so fair?
> Burghley says all the youth of England grow sick with love
> for her.

Leicester
You're fairer.

Elizabeth
She's younger.

Leicester
Is she? They say suffering has ruined her.
They say her flesh is grey – grey – we call it prison pallor.

Elizabeth
I'd love to know the truth – judge for myself – see her –

Leicester
See her then.
You may do as you please – you're our Queen. Your sun
    is at its height.
Burn her to cinders with the bright flames of your beauty –
Like Jupiter's glory consuming hapless Semele.
Watch her fade and wither like poppies sown among stones.

Elizabeth
Am I still beautiful? But no – I –

Leicester
Go to her.

Elizabeth
I forbid you to tempt me further.

Leicester
Only you can teach her what majesty should be.
Only you can show her what's she's thrown away.
If you appeared before her – a glorious vision –

Elizabeth
Never. It's impossible.

Slight pause.

I'll consult Burghley –

Leicester
Is Lord Burghley now Queen of England? When was
    Elizabeth deposed?
Be guided by me.

Elizabeth

If I give in to folly the fault will be mine, not yours . . .

Talk of my marriage has cast you down. I've hurt you.
Today I can deny you nothing. Tomorrow, no doubt, I'll
     change my mind.
But to see her – my almost sister!

I know how absolutely wisdom forbids it.
But then . . . wisdom forbids us everything.

Schiller says '**Leicester** *falls before his sovereign*' – *that is, throws
himself at her feet.* '*The curtain falls.*'

Act Three

A walled deer park. Beyond, the landscape seems to stretch, uninterrupted,
forever. Hunting horns in the distance. **Mary** *bounds on, exhilarated by*
her new-found freedom.

Mary
  The sun! The sun!
  See how the clouds sail free! Sail on, sail on!
  Carry my love to France – to freedom! I have no other
    messenger.

Kennedy *(hurrying after her, out of breath)*
  I'm too old for this –

Mary
  Grow young! Turn child again as I have done.
  Come out of the darkness into the light of heaven – look
    at the skies!
  The scent of morning upon the breeze – meadow-sweet
    and green grass –

Kennedy
  We're still not free –

Mary
  Free! –

Kennedy
  This deer park has high walls –

Mary
  Thank, thank the friendly trees for hiding them from me! –
  Don't speak of walls and prisons – let me imagine that just
    over that horizon –
  there where earth embraces heaven – I can see the
    mountains of my Scottish kingdom –
  Look – the blessed sun, warming my face – it's shining
    more brightly
  on the palaces of France. My beloved France! I see roads
    like ribbons

cut the clear blue skies, and all of them beckon me to
    freedom – freedom, freedom!

Kennedy

Just because Sir Amyas Paulet gives you leave to walk in
    the deer park –

Mary

No, Hannah, no. This is Leicester's doing – I know it,
    I know it!
For love of me he risks Elizabeth's displeasure – and this
    is only the beginning.
At first they will allow me small mercies, little privileges –
    then more and more –
bringing me by degrees to the idea of my release – and
    then, when my eyes
have grown accustomed to the light – when I see and
    know the world again –
they'll let me go. God's angel puts off my chains – throws
    open my prison doors.
Leicester!

Kennedy

Not many days ago they brought word of a death warrant –

Mary

And now it can never be signed.

Kennedy

They say that the condemned are often allowed a last taste
    of life.

The sounds of the hunt come nearer.

Mary

Croak, croak, says the raven! Doom, doom!

She laughs.

Can you hear the huntsmen! O what I'd give to gallop
    after them –
thundering down woodland paths – my horse's hooves
    throwing up clods of mud –

the stag bounding ahead in the dappled light – the music
of the hounds in full pursuit.

Enter **Paulet**.

Paulet
Now, Lady – Have I done well? Have I pleased you for once?

Mary
Sir Amyas?

Paulet
Don't I deserve your thanks?

Mary
For what? Then . . . Was it you who persuaded them –

Paulet
Who else, who else? I gave your letter to the Queen –

Mary
But –

Paulet
There were those who would have prevented me, but
I placed it in her hands myself –

Mary
And that is why she's granted me this freedom –

The hunting horns blow a kill.

Paulet
I've better news still. Do you hear those horns?

Mary (*realising*)
What of them?

Paulet
The Queen herself is with the hunt –

Mary
Oh!

Paulet
I assure you –

Mary (*going weak at the knees*)
Say it's not true –

Kennedy (*going to support her*)
Majesty –

Paulet
O but it is true! In a moment Queen Elizabeth will stand
before you.

Kennedy
Lady – My Lady – you're turning pale. Compose yourself –

Paulet
Is not this what you'd hoped – what you expected? Your
request seemed
clear enough to me – a meeting face to face. Well, now
you'll have it.

Kennedy
My Lady –

Paulet
In all my years I've never known her lost for words.

Kennedy
Pray God her language has not left her! Madame –

Paulet
She wished to plead before her peers and now Her Gracious
Majesty will hear her plea –

Mary
I am not yet ready!

Paulet
Come! You've had twenty years to prepare your case.

Mary
I'm not ready – the shock of it has stolen my breath –

Paulet
Must I repeat myself? It was your own request. I carried
it myself –

Mary
Hannah – help me back to the house. I need a moment
to think – to recover my –

Paulet
I can't permit it, Lady. You must stay here and face
the Queen.
It's your guilty soul makes you tremble before her.

Enter **Shrewsbury**, *hurriedly*. **Mortimer** *hangs back.*

Mary
God knows that's not the cause. He sees my innocence –
and knows . . .
Lord Shrewsbury?

He kisses her hand. **Paulet** *looks shocked.*

Shrewsbury
My Lady –

Mary
O my noble friend – my angel guardian – I am amazed
to see you here,
but thank God for you! I thank Him! My Lord, I cannot,
must not see her yet –

Shrewsbury
Lady, you must –

Mary
Prevent it, My Lord, I need time –

Shrewsbury
No, Lady, there is no time –

Mary
I need a priest – I feel such hatred, such anger –

Shrewsbury
Master it, Lady, master it –

Mary
I –

Shrewsbury
Speak softly, and with dignity.

Mary
Ten thousand times and more, in my imagination I've
spoken to her.
I've practised patience, searched out mild expressions,
schooled myself
in the language of reconciliation – learned soft answers
to turn away her wrath –
rehearsed my humbling scene until I have it by heart –
graven on my memory –
each tear – each tone . . . And now it's gone. I see it for
what it was: a playhouse speech –
hollow words and empty gestures. And I can't remember
a line of it. Gone – all gone.
My studied gentleness transforms into a timid hart – my
fury's a pack of hounds.
All I remember is my humiliation at her hands.

Shrewsbury
Then lash your hounds to heel. Let slip the true sweetness
of your nature.
If you fall prey to hatred then you're lost. Swallow down
your righteous anger.
Obey the time – kneel and beg her mercy.

Mary
I do not stoop, sir –

Shrewsbury
Do it!
A pardon – freedom is within your grasp! It's such a little
thing!
Speak firmly but respectfully – be yourself. She is by nature
compassionate –
thinks mercy a monarch's duty. Play upon her sympathy.
And, in the Name of God, say nothing of your injuries –
nothing of legality – the rights and wrongs of your
imprisonment –
that's for another day – once you're set at liberty.

Mary

For years I've prayed to God – begged Him for this meeting.
In answering my prayers He leads me to destruction.
Can fire blaze under water? Can the lamb command the
    tiger?
There can be no love between us – never, never, never.

Shrewsbury

You're wrong. I saw the tears in her eyes as she read
    your letter.
Lady, put aside your wrongs, and speak mildness to her.

Mary

O Shrewsbury, My dearest, dearest Lord.

She takes his hand.

If only they had let me stay your prisoner I would have
    been content.
I've been so harshly treated – harshness has hardened me –
I've vengeance in my heart where there should be
    forgiveness, patience, love –

Shrewsbury

Then call them back – forgiveness, patience love! Let
    vengeance go.
Now. Are you calmer?

Mary

Is Burghley with her?

Shrewsbury

No, no. Only the Earl of Leicester.

Mary

Leicester!

Shrewsbury

You've nothing to fear from him.
In public he's your enemy but privately I believe he speaks
    for your pardon.
Leicester persuaded the Queen to agree to this meeting.

Mary
Leicester! I knew it!

Shrewsbury
Knew what? What did you know?

Paulet
The Queen! The Queen!

Enter the hunting party, **Elizabeth** *and* **Leicester**. **Shrewsbury**
ushers away the huntsmen, who have blood on their hands, and
Elizabeth's *bodyguards.* **Paulet** *goes and kneels.*

Elizabeth
Sir Amyas.

She pretends she has just noticed **Mary**.

Elizabeth
Who is that lady?

Nobody dares reply.

Leicester
Your Majesty . . . You are at Fotheringhay . . .

He can't go on. She pretends to be shocked.

Elizabeth
Who is responsible for this act of folly? Leicester?

Leicester
Not folly, Majesty, but Divine Providence.
Heaven blesses a peacemaker – and bids us be merciful.
Let's pray for a joyful outcome.

Shrewsbury
Look graciously, Majesty, upon this wretched lady.
For too long she has shivered in the icy chill of your
    displeasure.

Elizabeth (*smiling*)
O has she so! Well, My Lords . . .
Which of you told me Lady Stuart was weighed down
by the heavy burden of her misfortunes?
I do not see her stoop. Is she still so disinclined to kneel to me?

Mary (*barely audible*)
Sister.

Going unsteadily towards **Elizabeth**, *she kneels.*

Mary
The bountiful heavens, that for so many years have smiled
  upon you,
set me here at your feet – a shipwreck of my former majesty
cast up by the tides of your measureless glory.
I bless your good fortune, Royal Lady,
and thank my God for it, who watches over both of us.

Pause. **Elizabeth** *doesn't move.*

Mary
Majesty.

Elizabeth *takes a step back.*

Mary
Don't leave me on my knees. But, of your grace, reach out
  a merciful hand,
to lift me from the depths of wretchedness. Pity my misery.

Elizabeth
I see you where God has placed you, Lady Mary. And
  I praise Him.
But for His grace I may have sunk so low.

Mary
He is quick to punish pride.
I love Him – honour Him who has shown me the
  worthlessness
of earthly sceptres, crowns, and painted pomp.
In changing my state from majesty to beggary
He teaches me to value truth, patience, and humility –
  How swiftly that change came!
Sister, I beg you, do not triumph in my downfall.
Honour the Tudor blood that runs in both our veins –
In showing mercy you raise our royal line – raising yourself
  with me.

Mercy's a God-given quality – in royalty it is the badge
   of heavenly glory.
I read nothing in your face.
O God in heaven!
My whole being clings to the frail wreckage of my words –
Do not be the rocks on which my hopes must founder!

Elizabeth
Choose your words carefully.
You have, in former times, insulted my majesty – I will
   not remember it.
You may think me a friend – a loving sister –
come here to comfort you – ignoring the wise counsel
   of my ministers,
who tell me mighty princes should never lower themselves
to consort with adulterers, and murderers.
You have leave to speak.

Mary
But how to begin!
Like you, I will not remember my former sorrows, nor
   chide the causers of them.
I have no wish to trouble you with petty injustice – the
   slights and insults
I have suffered, nor will I presume to lay them at your
   door. For I am sure –
had you known all I have endured there would have been
   a sudden end to my misery.
I am an anointed queen as you are – but in your kingdom
   long held a prisoner.
Dear God remove the venom from my words! –
Majesty, I mean no harm – I would not sting your ears
   with bitter accusation . . .
England has dealt harshly with me.
I came here a suppliant, but all I've seen of English
   hospitality
has been a mockery of what that sacred word should mean.

Shrewsbury
Lady –

Mary

No acknowledgement of my double royalty, my friends
    stripped from me,
cast into dungeons and infamy, set before spurious courts
    of enquiry –
But no, no! Let's not speak of that – let's not remember it.
Let's blame the stars – blame Fate – blame louring Fortune.
And most of all let's blame our high position.
A little, little quarrel between kings can scorch the earth,
their sins can sink whole nations.
And we – great princes in our lands – are fated to become
the only target of slanders, libels – the assassin's knife or
    madman's jealousies.

She approaches **Elizabeth** *more confidently – using an easier, more*
intimate tone.

Mary

But let it all go!
Let bitter remembrance fall away like tears.
We'll speak like sisters – without interpreters.
Come! Tell me, sister, everything of which I stand accused
and I will prove all accusations false – calm all your fears.
O if only we had spoken face to face – long, long ago –
    when first I came from France –
groundless suspicion would not have come between us!
We would neither of us have felt such awkwardness.

Elizabeth

Do you blame the stars? – you'd blame Fortune?
Yet I must thank my stars that save me
from the venomous darts hurled, in your name, at
    my person.
Why do you shuffle onto Destiny the guilty blows your
    family aim at me?
There was never any hostility towards you on my part.
I never called you anything but sister – cousin, friend –
No – though your uncle Cardinal Guise – that vicious
    hound of Rome,
ambitious for my crown, laid plots to steal my throne –

proclaiming you England's rightful Queen through all the
    courts of Europe –
seeking to incite rebellion here – even here in the heart
    of my peaceable kingdom.
How can you answer this? There is no answer. But while
    God stands at my side
all Rome's priestly soldiery are carried bleeding from the
    field.
Hell's legions aim at my head . . . It's your head on the block.

Mary
But cradled in the hands of God.
I cannot believe England would follow a course so bloody –

Elizabeth
Why shouldn't I? Answer me that, Lady.

Mary
The laws of nations – our God's commandments –

Elizabeth
A course so bloody! Your uncle Cardinal teaches me
    the way.
Have you never heard men speak of St Bartholomew's Day?
Yet every murder – every butchery is sanctified by that
    regicide in Rome –
that monstrous demon – triple whore of Babylon –
spewing his popish filth into my kingdom –
canonising my would-be assassins, blessing rebellion –
Why should I set you free? What oaths and sureties can you
    offer me?
What broken oath is there that Rome would not absolve
    and bless?
How can I bind you in chains of loyalty
when you think you can pick the locks with St Peter's keys?

Mary
You could name me, and James my son, your successors.
As God has set us in the line of succession, accept it.
And in accepting me accept my friendship –
together with that of every crowned head in Europe.

Elizabeth

My friendship's for me to give, not for you to take.
Do you think I'd pawn my nation to the Vatican? –
legitimise your claim to my throne?
Hurrying myself to an early grave while all the youth
    of England
clamour to see their golden idol crowned?

Mary

Then I renounce all claims!
God grant you and your people a long and prosperous reign!
Here before these witnesses I say it, and will sign:
Your kingdom is your own! – to have, to hold, to dispose
    of as you will.
I ask nothing – want nothing of yours.
My proud soul's lamed – a little bird trailing a broken wing.
    My song long silenced.
You see the shadow of a woman in her prime –
the faded image of a spirit smothered by years in prison . . .
Sister, have done with me. What have you come to say?
Don't toy so unkindly with my hopes and fears.

Elizabeth

What do you wish to hear? What would you have me say?
'Mary, I set you free. You that have felt the full force of
    my power,
now learn to bless me. I shall forgive your darkest
    conspiracy'?
Is that what you ask of me?

Mary

Give me only my life and freedom. I'll accept them as
    your gifts – not as of right, but of your mercy.
O say the words – end my agony!
For were our places changed I would not, for the wide
    world,
stand over you, looking down, as you look down on me.

Elizabeth

Our places changed? There's little hope of that now.
So – in the end you surrender the field to me?

Has all the fight gone out of you? Yes, I see it has.
My moon grows full and yours is on the wane.
Poor wounded thing! Are there no more champions to
    enter the lists for you?
No more assassins to strike me down for love of you?
Is there no husband waiting to wed you?
No lust-crazed singing-boy to lure into your bed –

Mary

Sister! Sister! O God! God! Have you no shame?

Elizabeth

What do you think, My Lords?
Do you see anything in her looks to drive a young man mad?
Well, Lady – I was told no woman would stand, willingly,
    at your side
for fear of being cast in shadows by the brightness of your
    beauty.
She disappoints me, Leicester.
I can only think her attraction's like that of a bitch on heat,
irresistible to all the dogs in town –

Mary

I'll not bear this!

Elizabeth

I think you must! (*Laughs.*)
Oho we'll see her real face now –
Off comes the mask of tragedy!

Mary (*with her fury in control, and great dignity*)

I thank my God, who knows my every fault,
my sins are not one half so black as the world paints them.
Nobody has felt the shame of failure more keenly that I –
my follies are the common gossip of firesides and taverns –
exposed to the judgement of every fool in Christendom.
Yet my greatest sins were little more than youthful error –
I placed a childlike trust in brutal, cunning men who used
    me and threw me down.
And what I have since gained of virtue is acknowledged
    by no man.
But, woman, what does the world say of you?

Leicester
Madame –

Mary
If ever that thinnest of veils that hides your baseness is
    torn away –

Shrewsbury (*interposing himself between them*)
Dear God in heaven! Is this the mildness you promised,
    Lady?

Mary
Mildness to the devil! No, I'll suffer her no longer –

Shrewsbury
It's her madness that speaks – Majesty, forgive her!

Leicester
Elizabeth – Majesty, come with me. Shut your ears to
    her fury –

But **Elizabeth** *seems petrified – mesmerised by* **Mary**'*s natural authority.*

Mary
Though all your people mock you, I never have.
I never called you bastard.
That was your father, and his Privy Council –
the whole of Europe, and His Holiness the Pope
called you that shameful name – setting it down in bulls
    and Acts of Parliament.

Nor did I call your mother whore.
That was your father too –
and if ever a man knew a whore it was your father –
He it was, and all your loyal subjects, and the world
heaped upon her that more than shameful title – a blister
    on your blood.
No, I never called her whore, nor you bastard.

Until this day.

But so I call you now! – Usurper too, and traitor to my
    throne.
What are you but vulgarity's minion – your people's puppet?

A wooden face, painted thick to hide duplicity,
Old whore to Lord Burghley's policy, heir to your mother's
    trade and treachery –
Unfit to rule, despised by all . . . Unloved!
Sink in the dirt before your rightful Queen!
Dirt is your destiny, for out of the dirt you came!

Elizabeth *exits fast, then the lords follow her in the height of confusion.*

Kennedy
So that's the end of us.

Mary
What joy! It's over! Over, Hannah! Our long captivity!
    What joy!

Kennedy
What madness! –

Mary
She was *furious*! O her face! – She'll kill me! But I've won!
    Victory! Victory!

Kennedy
You are mad –

Mary
I feel so light! – the burden of all those endless years –
    just slipping away –

Kennedy
What were you thinking? To insult her – and in front
    of her lover –

Mary
Isn't it wonderful! O I was magnificent!
To crush her like that while he stood and laughed – urging
    me to do it –

Kennedy
I never saw him laughing.

Mary
Inside he was laughing!

Mortimer (*coming forward*)
  You *are* magnificent, Lady – that was true majesty.
  You taught her what it is to be a queen! – a goddess! –

Mary
  Mortimer! You saw it all! You saw My Lord? Did you
    give him my letter – my picture?

Mortimer
  What beauty! What flames of passion! –

Mary
  Tell me quickly, sir. What did he say? –

Mortimer
  Forget him! Forget him – a liar and a coward –
  too timid to play his part – forget him!

Mary
  But –

Mortimer
  He's worthless – unfit to carry a sword.

Mary
  Did you give him my letter?

Mortimer
  Too fond of his wretched life to risk it in your service –
  He'll dare nothing – Nothing! But what does Leicester
    matter?
  If I had a thousand lives I'd lay them down for you –
  I'm the only one – your last and only hope –

Kennedy
  Don't come near her!

Mortimer
  Tonight! – tonight I'll set you free –

Mary
  But how? How!

Mortimer

Twelve of us – we strike tonight – the priest has heard our
last confessions –
absolved us of the sin of shedding blood –

Mary

No –

Mortimer

Upon the body of Our Saviour we're sworn to save you –

Mary

I'll have no more bloodshed –

Mortimer

The Pope himself has washed us clean of it –

Mary

But your uncle – Sir Amyas –

Mortimer

I'll kill him myself – they'll all die. The Pope has blessed
the deed!

Mary

I forbid it! It's too terrible to think upon.

Mortimer

And if I have to kill Elizabeth that blow is blessed in heaven –

Mary

But not by me!
You'll go no further with this – it's madness.
There's not the slightest chance of success! Twelve men!
You'll all be killed –

Mortimer

What does it matter? My love for you –

Mary

Love!

Mortimer

I love you – I'm in love with you! What is a life! What are
twelve lives!
O sweetest Lady –

Mary

No – don't touch me! Hannah!

Mortimer

Such scorn – why do you look on me with contempt?
    What's wrong with me?
Am I not high enough for you – not royal – not man
    enough?
How high was young David Rizzio –

Mary

Dear God, dear God!

Kennedy

Come away from him!

Mortimer

You've had many lower lovers – I'm sent to you by heaven –

Mary

Don't touch me!

Mortimer

It's God's will – I can't help myself. Let me hold you –

He forces himself upon her. She struggles. Shouts in the distance – several shots.

Mary

Help me! Help me! God!

Kennedy

Soldiers! Soldiers! There are soldiers everywhere! What's
    happening!

Mortimer

I'll protect you!

He draws his sword. **Paulet** *rushes on at the head of a band of soldiers.* **Mary** *and* **Kennedy** *escape towards the house.*

Paulet

Where is she? Get her inside! Follow her – quickly, quickly!

Mortimer

Uncle! What's happening?

Paulet

Assassins! Catholics! Get Mary under lock and key. The
Queen is dead –
struck down at the gates of the park!

Mortimer

Which Queen –

Paulet

Our Queen, you fool! Queen Elizabeth! She's dead!

They all rush off. Noise and confusion, shots.

Act Four

The Palace of Westminster – an antechamber.

Sombre mood. **Aubespine**, *French lords waiting. Enter from the inner chamber* **Burghley**, **Davison**, *the* **Earl of Kent**, *and others.* **Shrewsbury** *and* **Leicester** *are absent.*

Burghley
I have drafted the order for Mary's execution. Here.

Giving notes.

Prepare the warrant for signature and sealing. There's not a moment to be lost.

Davison
I'll have it copied fair.

He exits.

Aubespine
My Lords, what can I say? My mind's in turmoil –
Am I awake or asleep? Is this a nightmare or are these things really happening?

Burghley
O they're happening, M'sieur Ambassador.

Aubespine
Struck down in the midst of her loyal subjects! How!
How could it happen?

Burghley
Struck by a Frenchmen, sir.

Aubespine
A madman?

Burghley
A papist, sir. A priest. A devil.

Kent
All papists are madmen, sir.

Aubespine
May God cast him into hottest flames of hell.

Burghley
Amen to that, sir. And with him all those who put him
up to it.
Here are letters for your King. You must leave England
at once.

Aubespine
Oh? Lord Burghley, my King has not recalled me. Until –

Burghley
Your office protects you until tomorrow. After that I cannot
vouch for you safety –

Aubespine
But what are you saying? Am I accused of some –

Burghley
Better not to ask, sir. Once brought to light, your crimes
could never be forgiven.

Aubespine
Let me remind you, sir, I am the voice of the King of
France –

Burghley
Are you saying your King encouraged these assassins?

Aubespine
I'm saying no such thing!

Burghley
Then don't attempt to hide behind His Majesty's skirts, sir.
The murderer's letters of safe conduct were written in
your hand –

Aubespine
As are all such conducts! Can I see into the heart of every
Frenchman in London,
or know his hidden purposes?

Burghley

A priest, sir – who heard confession and said Mass in your
own house!

Aubespine

My house is open to all my countrymen.

Burghley

To all England's enemies!

Aubespine

I refuse to leave Court until this matter has been thoroughly
investigated –

Burghley

It has been. The evidence damns you.

Aubespine

In insulting me, sir, you insult the majesty of France!
Would you endanger the treaty we have signed? The
marriage –

Burghley

There is no treaty. I threw it on the fire myself. There will
be no marriage.
Arrest him, Lord Marshall, see he's sent packing before
morning.

Kent

With pleasure, My Lord.

Enter **Leicester**.

Burghley

Best hold him here until nightfall, then under guard to
Dover.

Aubespine

My house –

Burghley

You have no house, sir.
The London mob is up. We found your papers, and the
weapons you had stored,

then the citizens took it upon themselves to burn your
residence to the ground.

Aubespine

My King will have your head, sir!

Burghley

Will he come and take it himself, or send his mincing
catamites to pluck it off?

Aubespine

Oh!

Kent

Come, sir.

Exeunt **Kent, Aubespine** *and French lords.*

Burghley

Leicester, you are forbidden to leave Court.

Leicester

By whom?

Burghley

By order of the Privy Council.
We wish to satisfy ourselves you had no hand in this
business –

Leicester

I –

Burghley

It was you persuaded Her Majesty to go to Fotheringhay.
No others of the Council knew of it, and at Fotheringhay
assassins lay in wait.

Leicester

Lord Shrewsbury knew –

Burghley

Lord Shrewsbury, poor, deluded fool, was always Mary's
friend.
Why this sudden change of heart in you, My Lord?
You'd have us believe you're Mary's enemy,
why then did you plan this secret meeting with the Queen?

At the very least you exposed Her Majesty to insults of
such –

Leicester
Wretched, worthless drudge! I'll teach you to know your
betters! I am an Earl!
Come with me – now! Accuse me in the Council –

Burghley
O I will! Depend upon it. And when I do, be sure your
answers are sufficient.

He goes back into the inner chamber.

Leicester
I'm lost – he knows, he knows! I'm a dead man. All
circumstances are against me.
If they find out I've exchanged letters with Mary –

Enter **Sir Amyas Paulet** *with a box of papers, followed by*
Mortimer. **Paulet** *goes into the inner chamber.* **Mortimer** *hangs
back.*

Leicester
No! No – this is your doing! Keep away from me!

Mortimer
The hounds are after me – they're on my trail – it's only
a matter of time –

Leicester
What's that to me? –

Mortimer
Yours too – they'll sniff you out. They took cartloads of
letters from Aubespine's house – they'll soon know we
planned everything from there.

Leicester
I've had no dealings with Aubespine –

Mortimer
The assassin was our priest – but he wanted all the glory
for himself –
he struck too early. Leicester, you must help me –

Leicester

I'll have nothing to do with you –

Mortimer

Listen to me, coward!

Leicester

For the love of God, lower your voice!

Mortimer

My uncle found Queen Mary's hiding place – copies of all the letters she's written –

Leicester

How could she be so feckless! She –

Mortimer

There are letters to you!

Leicester

What!

Mortimer

Imploring you not to desert her –

Leicester

God! No –

Mortimer

Promising you her hand in marriage –

Leicester

Jesu! –

Mortimer

Begging you to kiss the picture she sent –

Leicester

I am a dead man!

Mortimer

My uncle's given Burghley the letters. He'll be reading them now –

Leicester

A dead man.

Mortimer
Your only course is to seize power –

Leicester
You're insane –

Mortimer
Act while you're still at liberty – why should Burghley have
    control? –
You outrank him don't you? Arrest him then – in the
    Council – swear the treason's his.
You're a soldier, the Queen's favourite, her guard will
    obey you.
For once in your wretched life be a man! I can do no more.
My friends are killed or taken – I must make a run for
    France.
Only you can save Mary – God help her! – get her away
    in the confusion.
You must seize power! Act – now – before we're all lost.

Leicester
You're right – I will! I must! Guards! Guards!

Enter at least three soldiers.

Guards. Arrest this traitor – watch him closely – he's a
    Catholic and a conspirator.
I'll inform Her Majesty.

Mortimer
O fool! Fool! Fool!
To trust a –

He draws his sword and attacks **Leicester**.

Mortimer
– painted harlot's bauble,
a woman's plaything – bastard's minion –

Officer
Cut his legs – slash at his arms –

They cut his legs from under him.

Mortimer

Ah, slaves! Traitors to Christ – His Mother!
You serve a usurping whore – a bastard! – damned for
  eternity!

Leicester

Bind him! Stop his mouth!

Mortimer

Holy Mary pray for me! Take me to heaven's glories!

Stabs himself as the guards overpower him.

Officer

Papist! Devil! Traitor!

Mortimer

I'd be all those things – before I'd be Leicester!

He dies.

Elizabeth*'s private apartments.* **Burghley** *has just handed her a
few letters which she is reading.* **Paulet** *stands by.*

Elizabeth

A wild and downward blow – entangled in the thick fur
  of my hunting cloak.
I took a scratch – a bruising. But had not Shrewsbury been
  more agile than his years . . .

Burghley

Lord Shrewsbury struck down the assassin?

Elizabeth

He warded the blows, until my guard could shoot the
  villain . . .
Dear God! But here's worse treason! Leicester!
O Burghley, never was woman more deeply betrayed.
To lead me in triumph – to couple me with his whore –

Burghley

Yet I cannot, for the life of me, imagine how he persuaded
you to it, Madame.

After all my warnings. Sir Amyas, you may go.

Exit **Paulet**.

Elizabeth

O my shame! They're laughing at me, Burghley – laughing!
Was ever woman so wickedly abused!

Burghley

In future, you may set a higher value upon my counsel.

Elizabeth

I should have followed it – in everything. Now I'm punished
for my wilfulness.

But Leicester, Leicester! Where can I hide my heart now
he proves false?

O the ingratitude of the man! I raised him highest of
you all –

almost to the level of my crown – allowing him to strut
before you like a king!

Burghley

Yet he abandons you for a queen of whores.

Elizabeth

Nobody abandons me. Have you the warrant?

Burghley

I've drafted it. Davison is copying it fair.

Elizabeth

Hurry him on – she must die tonight.

Leicester shall witness her death. Then let him linger a
month or two,

before he follows her to the block. Do you suppose they'll
laugh at me then?

My love is dead.

There is an empty chamber in my heart – once it was his.
I'll lodge my vengeance there to fill the void.

Living, he was my weakness displayed to the wide-eyed
world.
His death will a be monument to my terrible strength.
Have the Earl of Leicester removed to the Tower, Burghley,
then nominate the peers
who'll sit in judgement on him.

Burghley
I'll give it some thought.

Elizabeth
But do it now.

Burghley
You know he'll plead with you −

Elizabeth
How? What can he say? His guilt's set down in black and
white.

She throws the letters.

Burghley
I fear you'll pity him −

Elizabeth
I'll never see his face again. I want him in the Tower.

Page
The Earl of Leicester.

Elizabeth
What insolence! The devil himself would be more welcome.
Tell the traitor he's forbidden the presence!

Page
Your Majesty, I dare not! He'll never believe you mean it −

Elizabeth
Get out! I've raised him so high these creatures obey him
and question my own commands. Out!

Burghley
Tell the Earl Her Majesty will not see him.

Exit **Page**, *worried.*

Elizabeth
O but could we be wrong! Am I misjudging him?

Burghley
He's a traitor –

Elizabeth
Her letters prove it – But –

Burghley
There is no 'but', Madame –

Enter **Leicester** *pushing the* **Page** *in front of him, with the*
Officer of the Guard *and two soldiers.*

Leicester
If I am barred the Court I'll hear it from your own mouth,
    Elizabeth.
(*To the* **Page** *and soldiers.*) Outside! Wait at the door –

Elizabeth
Manifest treason!

Leicester
You'll hear Burghley, so you'll hear me. Do you think I'll
    cower and cringe while this –
this creature of ink and paper blackens my name with lies?

Burghley
My Lord! Remember where you are!

Leicester
Remember you stand before your betters, Mr Secretary –
Speak only when I bid you speak – Leave us!
And as for you, Lady, nobody – nobody! – forbids the Earl
    of Leicester
access to his Sovereign. If I'm disgraced then speak it to
    my face!

Elizabeth
You disgrace yourself! Get out of my sight!

Burghley
That's plain enough –

Leicester
You heard me, Burghley! Out of my sight!

Elizabeth
Stay, Burghley!

Leicester
Out! There are some loving words I'd speak to this woman,
we want no eavesdroppers nor peeping Toms –

Elizabeth
O he's proud!

Leicester
As Lucifer, Madame –

Elizabeth
Lucifer fell!

Leicester
From the skies! If I aspire to heaven, then you have set
    me there –
You raised me to the heights with whispered words of love.

Elizabeth
Leicester –

Leicester
Lifting me above the jostling crowds of petty lords and
    servile councillors.
I will defend the love you've given me,
and challenge all that would dislodge me from your heart.
Dismiss that unnecessary man – I've things to say to you
    he must not hear.

Elizabeth
You will no longer baffle my heart with words. Read this
    letter.

Leicester
O I guess what this is. From the Stuart woman?

Elizabeth
How can you deny your guilt? You have her portrait!

Leicester
Yes. Here.

He throws it down.

Elizabeth
You promised her your love – even your hand in marriage –
Swore you would work in secret to contrive her escape –

Leicester
What of it?

Burghley
What of it! You confess – you confess!

Leicester
Why should I deny it?

Elizabeth
From his own mouth –

Burghley
Shameless villain –

Elizabeth
Out of my sight! Send him to the Tower –

Burghley
Barefaced traitor –

Leicester
Call me a traitor and you'll die, Burghley. All I have done,
    I have done –
and everything was to protect our Queen.

Elizabeth
A riddle!

Burghley
No Delphic puzzling can alter the facts –

Leicester
That I've saved her life!

Elizabeth
Mine!

Leicester
Yours! The world knows I detest Mary Stuart –
How often have I urged her execution?
Yet when I saw how stubbornly you set your face against
her death
I went to work in secret to flush out her treachery –

Burghley
Why in secret? If you knew –

Leicester
I would have thought Burghley the last of all men
to need a lecture from me on the value of secrecy.
Is he not the most secret of secretaries –
a black spider lurking in a web of policy?
But had it not been for me, Mary, as we speak,
would have been over the border in Scotland –
or gathering troops in France, or inciting invasion from
Philip of Spain.
Burghley's intelligence failed him.

Burghley
Idle boasts, preposterous fictions –

Leicester
Then tell me this – let's speak some more of secrets –
Did not Your Majesty try and suborn Sir Amyas Paulet –
that simple, loyal man – to have his prisoner murdered?

Elizabeth and **Burghley** *exchange guilty glances.*

Leicester
And, when he refused, did you not go to work on his
nephew, Mortimer?

Burghley
Why do you make these accusations?

Leicester
Because I know they're true!

Burghley for all his spies was unaware
the young man was a fanatic – an assassin in the pay
   of Cardinal Guise –
at the heart of the plot to free Mary and kill our Queen –

Burghley
Laughable!

Elizabeth (*shocked*)
Young Mortimer?

Leicester
He was the cunning messenger who carried her witchcraft
   here –
thinking to seduce me to her cause. I led them on.
And when the time was right – tonight they would have
   struck –
I got in a first blow. I arrested him –

Elizabeth
Everybody plots against me –

Burghley
Bring him before us – we'll hear it from his own mouth.

Leicester
The traitor's dead.

Elizabeth
Mortimer?

Burghley
He's alive! I saw him – minutes ago.

Leicester
Killed himself. As the Queen's guards arrested him –

Burghley
O I see! I see! So now he cannot deny the treason you'd
   smear him with?
He died by his own hand – or was it yours, My Lord?

Leicester
Slow-witted, slanderer – Guard! Captain!

Enter **Officer**.

Leicester
Tell Her Majesty how Mortimer died.

Officer
Your Majesty.

Elizabeth
You may speak.

Officer
He came here with his uncle, Madame, enquiring for
    His Lordship here.
We were on duty, outside your chamber door. I heard
    My Lord's voice raised in anger.
We went to find the traitor Mortimer, with drawn sword,
    attacking My Lord –
and heaping such filthy slanders on Your Majesty's name –

Leicester
No more of that.

Officer
We overpowered the young man – but not before he'd
    stabbed himself.
He died in our arms.

Leicester
Thank you, Captain. You've leave to go.

Officer
Your Majesty. My Lord.

Elizabeth
I'm lost in darkness – wandering in a maze –

Leicester
I saved your life. Left to Burghley we'd have a Stuart on
    your throne,
the Pope and his Inquisition holding court in Westminster,
    and High Mass
sung in every parish church.

Elizabeth

In this world of deceit how may I find truth?
How can I believe you? How not believe you?
Love and guilt are in the balance –
And that wicked woman's the scale of all my wretchedness!

Leicester

Then cut her head off.

Elizabeth

No – no! (*Slight pause.*)
You will do it.

Leicester

Me!

Burghley

What better way to free yourself of suspicion?

Elizabeth

They are drawing up the death warrant. We charge you
with overseeing her execution.
I place the whole matter in your hands – see the sentence
carried out.

Burghley

These letters suggest that the woman was your lover.

Elizabeth

Your commission is to kill her. Wash away all suspicion
of love for her.

Burghley

Do you accept the commission?

Leicester

It's not fit work for an Earl . . . One of my birth and
station . . .
But since it is the wish of Her Majesty – since she deems
it necessary
that I should prove once more my love and loyalty – I'll do it.

Elizabeth

Fetch me the warrant. Burghley will assist you.

Burghley

It will be a pleasure to do so.

Exit **Burghley**. *Enter* **Kent**.

Elizabeth

What now, Kent?

Kent

The citizens of London, Your Majesty, press to the palace
gates.

Elizabeth

What do they ask?

Kent

To see you, Majesty.
Wild rumour proclaims you dead – that the papists have
freed Mary and will set a Catholic on your throne.
They're calling for her execution.
I think you should go to them.

Elizabeth

So the citizens of London wish to command their Queen.
The world's turned upside down!

Enter **Davison**.

Elizabeth

What now?

Davison

The warrant, Majesty. For Mary Stuart's execution.

Elizabeth (*recoiling as if in horror from it*)

Dear God! Vile thing! Set it down.

Enter **Burghley** *and* **Shrewsbury**.

Burghley

Sign it, Your Majesty, and I'll set the seal to it. Your people
will have the matter settled –

Elizabeth

My people! Today they clamour for her death – Who knows
if tomorrow they will not shout for mine? –

Fickle, fickle people! When she's dead they'll pity her –
forever crying for a thing, then crying because they have it.
You see, Shrewsbury! See how they force me to it!

Shrewsbury

No one can force Your Majesty. You need do nothing you
do not wish.
And certainly nothing should be done while the mob rules
the street,
and confusion clouds good judgement. Let the Londoners
disperse.
Let your own anger cool. Do nothing. The power is in
your hands.
Time is your own. Do nothing.

Burghley

Sign the warrant.

Kent

A sight of you will send the people home.

Elizabeth

My will is not my own.

Burghley

You must sign.

Shrewsbury

At least pause – give me time to dissuade you from this
dangerous course.
Consider, Madame. The warrant lies here on the table.
For twenty years your conscience has prevented you from
setting your hand to it.
A little stroke – a flourish of the pen – and you've usurped
the prerogative of heaven
to save or punish one of the Lord's anointed.
Consider. Should you in a moment of terror – in the midst
of this confusion –
give yourself to an error twenty years of sober reflection
could not draw you to?
Do nothing in the heat. We'll talk of it tomorrow.

Burghley

No! The heat's too great. While you dither and delay the
building burns –

Tomorrow the whole kingdom could be in flames!

Elizabeth

I'm in God's hands!

Shrewsbury

God strengthen my voice as He did my arm when the
madman struck at you.

In the midst of earthquake, wind, and fire, Majesty, hear
the still small voice of reason.

Do you fear to let Mary live? Think how much greater
will be your fear if Mary dies.

She will rise, a Fury, from the grave you lay her in, screaming
injustice, terror and revenge.

Scotland and France will remember she was their Queen.

In Rome, the Pope will pronounce her martyrdom – his
instrument will be Philip of Spain . . .

Many of your people love the old religion – their hearts
are torn in two.

Loving what you destroy they'll turn on you, remembering
she comes of a line of English kings –

all this will make them pity her.

Elizabeth

I pity her myself!

Shrewsbury

Today the people love you – and hate her. But stir up
unrest – thrust them into war –

and see how they'll greet you then as you ride through
London's streets.

You'll feel how soon their love grows cold: a chill – an
icy wind.

Where now they kneel to you, cheering and shouting the
warmth of their blessings,

you'll hear jeers and curses – like one dragged to her
execution.

Elizabeth

O Shrewsbury, Shrewsbury! Would I were in my grave!

Why did you ward the assassin's friendly blow that would
  have laid me there –

out of this world of cares? Let her have her life! Let her
  have my throne! –

I am unequal to the majesty my father thrust upon me.

As God is my witness, I never wished it. Or let my people
  rule –

they'd lead me – jostle me into every act of folly vulgar
  imagination ever dreamed upon!

Well, offer them my sceptre – take my crown! God sees my
  heart – He knows

I never wanted rule and sway – only my country's good.
  Let me hide myself away –

I am unfit for sovereignty. Why should I steer the ship of
  destiny,

when every man thinks he could sail it better? Let more
  brutal hands attempt it!

Try as I might, I cannot force my heart to cruelty. My
  people think only of their own happiness, but they'd
  have me pay for it with a life of wretchedness.

Burghley

By the nails and cross of Christ Our Saviour! Let there
  be an end to this woman's folly!

You think I speak treason? It's treason to say nothing in
  the face of your rambling!

Give the people your throne and sceptre? Give it to that
  creature of Rome?

Show us some glimmer of kingly determination, and be
  not for ever hiding

behind selfish womanly weakness, and tears of policy!

Would you abandon the English Church,

given to us by your great father and your brother?

Shall your council chambers become monks' cloisters?

Would you have Parliament, and your loyal ministers,

kneel to the papal legate – as they did in your sister's
  bloody reign?

On the souls of your people, given into your faltering care
    by the hand of God,
I demand Mary Stuart's head! Now, will you sign the death
    warrant?
Your country's salvation hangs on your answer.
Would you cast us all into hell and damnation?
Let's hear no more of effeminate compassion –
you're the servant of your country. In God's name, do
    your duty!

Elizabeth (*mildly*)

I shall, My Lords. Now leave me. I will pray for God's
    guidance.
No human counsel can assist me in this terrible ordeal.
God's will be done, and never my own.

They go out. **Shrewsbury** *looks pitifully at her.*

Elizabeth

Davison. Wait outside the door.

He exits.

Why do I call myself a queen that know myself no better
    than a slave –
a fool to my loutish people, my murmuring courtiers, and
    to Fortune?
My people! – why should I care whether they smile or
    frown on me?
I judge their cloying love contemptible.
I loathe the flattery of my court, but can do nothing
to free myself from the crushing embrace of Fate.
When shall I rule England as I please?
Leicester, Burghley, Shrewsbury . . . they're no longer
    afraid of me.
I cannot awe them as my father did – crush their rebellious
    hearts.
He ruled by fear – I traded kingly tyranny for a vision of
    Justice –
and what a fleeting, useless vision it has proved!
Has Justice protected me from the assaults of anti-Christ –

the scorn of France – the threats of Catholic Spain?
Has Justice won for me my people's love and loyalty?
Has Justice silenced their whisperings of my bastardy?
I am one woman. I stand alone against the world.

But *she* will not stand by me – I will not let Mary live to
    see me stoop.
She is the adder lying in my path – striking at every step
    I hope to take,
poisoning my hopes of France, setting Leicester and myself
    at stinging odds.
All blows of misfortune I have ever borne were struck
    by Mary Stuart.
They carry her stamp and name . . .

But it will be *my* name – my seal on her death warrant.
Then I'm free of her – free as breeze that plays upon the
    mountain tops.
With what contempt she stared at me, as if her pride could
    strike me to the ground.
Her blows are weak.
My mother a whore? And I'm a bastard?

She picks up her pen.

This is a killing stroke. And it's legitimate.

*She signs. She is then horrified by what she has done. After a moment she
calls:*

Davison!

He enters.

Davison
My Lady?

Elizabeth
Where are the Lords?

Davison
At the palace gates – speaking to the citizens.

Elizabeth
The mob. I suppose I shall have to show myself –

wave and nod to them, smile graciously: 'I thank you, my
loving people – I thank you!'
My people! Greasy filth and scum!
Leave us.

He starts to go.

O . . . And take the warrant you brought along with you.
'*In manus tuas, Domine, commendo spiritum meum.*'

She hands him the warrant.

Davison
Yes, Your Majesty . . . But, My Lady . . . ! It's signed.

Elizabeth
You brought it to be signed. I have signed it.

Davison
Yes, Your Majesty.

Elizabeth
Though whilst in your care it remains a harmless paper.
Harmless as a sonnet.

Davison
Your Majesty –

Elizabeth
Only when it's given up will it be transformed into a
bloody instrument.
Whilst in your hand, my name on it is innocent.

Davison
But your signature makes all the difference.
The difference between life and death for the Queen
of Scotland.
The commissioners – the sheriff of the county – and the
executioners
will set to work as soon as the document is delivered.

Elizabeth
Then I pray to God that you understand your duty.

She starts to leave.

Davison
But, Majesty – I *don't* understand.
Do you wish me to hold back the warrant, or serve it
    immediately?

She looks at him.

No, no, My Lady! I beg you – make it clear to me –
what would you have me do?
How am I to interpret your intentions?
This business is deadly – tell me how I am to proceed.
Am I to set in motion the terrible machinery?

She turns her back on him.

Surely you cannot expect me to decide the matter?
Royal Majesty – all I have ever known is loyal service.
Give me clear orders and I'll obey them – I always have –
but I'm no politician – no judge, no executioner.
The slightest slip in this is death – worse! – any error in
    the business is regicide!
I'm merely your servant – tell me what I must do?

She says nothing.

I beg you – don't go! You've told me nothing!
I'm to proceed at once – it's merely that you can't bring
    yourself to say the words?
Is that it? Have I guessed your mind?

She frowns at him.

Dear God, dear God! Then I'm to keep the warrant? Yes?
Retain it until you judge the time is right?
A single word – a gesture! For the love of God,
make clear your intentions!
Royal Lady!

She refuses to respond.

I've not been long in office – I'm new to the ways of the
    Court –
If only you'd tell me what I'm doing wrong – forgive me
    my ignorance.

I'm a plain man. All I do is carry out another's wishes.
  I obey commands.
What am I to do?

No response.

Then take it back! For the love of my soul I want no
  part in it!
Take it back – it burns my fingers like hot coals!
For God's love say! What are your wishes!

Elizabeth
  I wish never to hear of the matter again. Don't fail me
  in this.

She exits.

Davison
  God help me! O God help me!

He falls on his knees and starts to pray. Enter **Burghley**.

Davison
  O My Lord! Thank God you've come!

Burghley
  What is it, man?

Davison
  You appointed me to this office –
  I pray you now dismiss me – at once. I'm not capable
  of it –
  I don't want it – it will be the death of me –

Burghley
  Control yourself, Davison! What has the Queen said
  to you?

Davison
  Nothing! Nothing – she'll say nothing! She signed the
  warrant and she –

Burghley
  She's signed it!

Davison
But she –

Burghley
Thank God who made her see sense! – Give it to me at
once.

Davison
I can't! I dare not!

Burghley
What are you saying?

Davison
She's left everything unclear. I must not hand it over –
and yet I must –

Burghley
Then why would she sign it? Surely that's enough –

Davison
O God, God! What am I to do!

Burghley
Give it to me!

Davison
I'll be damned for it!

Burghley *snatches for it.*

Burghley
I'll see you damned if you don't give me it! Fool!

He forces it out of **Davison**'s *hand.*

Burghley (*going*)
There's not a moment to be lost. I must apply the seal,
then on to its bloody conclusion at Fotheringhay.

Davison
No, stop! She ordered me to keep it safe –

Burghley
It's too late now. Go tell her you've delivered it.

He goes. **Davison** *follows him.*

Davison

I dare not! Where are you going, My Lord! My Lord!
Tell me what I should do! Wait!

Act Five

The same as Act One. But the room is piled high with objects of silver and gold, paintings, mirrors, all objects belonging to **Mary** *which have now been returned. Guards bring in more objects, including pictures of members of* **Mary**'s *family.* **Margaret Kurl** *replaces the canopy over* **Mary**'s *throne, then goes out. Other ladies at work. Everybody wears black.* **Hannah Kennedy** *has been weeping.* **Paulet** *hands* **Kennedy** *a box of jewellery and an inventory and leaves. Enter* **Melville**, **Mary**'s *old steward, who was removed from her many years previously.*

Kennedy
Melville! I never thought to see you again.

Melville
They've allowed me to visit her for the last time –

Kennedy
O God! You're here to –

Melville
Yes, I've come to bid Our Lady farewell. The time that's
    left to me on earth
I'll spend in mourning her.

Kennedy
She will be glad of you. We've had so little time to prepare.
Young Mortimer talked wildly of escape – and, in the
    night, when we heard the noise – the hammering – we
    thought . . .
I began to hope. But it was the carpenters – at work in
    the room below us –

Melville
Building the scaffold. Yes, I saw.

Kennedy
Once I held a child in my arms. The changes, day by day,
    year upon year,
by which she came to womanhood, I hardly noted in her.
    She was a babe.

She was a woman − a royal queen. But now she's to be
    brought to her death.
She'll be gone in a moment − the blinking of an eye.

Melville
And in the next she'll be with us in eternity.

Kennedy
When she heard them at work in the room below, God
    granted her the strength
to look death in the face. She's stronger than all of us −
    no word of complaint,
no shudder of terror . . . It was only when they told her
    of Leicester's deep betrayal,
and the death of that poor, misguided young man . . . Only
    then she shed for them
a tear or two. Not one for herself.

Kurl *comes back with a goblet of wine.*

Kennedy
Put it on the table.

Kurl
Can it be Melville? Our Lady's steward −

Melville
Yes, Margaret, yes −

Kurl
Dear old friend! Have you come from London?

Melville
I have come from Rome − but yes. I've been in London.

Kurl
Have you news of my wretched husband?

Melville
They say Elizabeth will release him from the Tower, once −

Kurl
You were going to say 'once Our Lady is dead'.

Melville
Yes.

Kurl

You know it was his testimony condemned her? His and
   Claude Nau's.

I couldn't believe it of him – disloyal, treacherous,
   despicable –

Melville

Lady, we do not know how they worked upon him.

Kurl

Destruction take his soul. He is a liar – he lied on oath.

Melville

Yet do not curse your husband –

Kurl

I'll cry it in the streets – in London – in Elizabeth's face
   at Westminster –

my husband's a liar! My Lady dies innocent – I know it!

Melville

God grant her His grace.

Kurl

I'll take her this wine. It will give her a little strength. She
   says she needs nothing,

but I'll not have her look pale when . . .

She sinks down.

O God! I've seen it – I looked into the room.

Kennedy

What have you seen?

Kurl

The scaffold – hung with black. The block itself. The
   headsman's axe.

The room is full of people – and the worse thing to my
   mind:

they're talking of everyday things. No concern for us – for
   Our Lady –

neither vengeful, nor angry, nor pitying – just – talking of
   little things . . .

While in a few moments we must –

Kennedy
That's enough. The Queen is coming.

Enter **Mary**. *She is dressed in white – the traditional French Court mourning – but she looks more like a bride. She wears an Agnus Dei at her breast, a rosary at her waist, and holds a crucifix in her hands. They kneel to her, in tears.*

Mary
Still in tears? Have I not forbidden them?
What use to me are tears, on this happiest of days?
The long dark night of cold captivity, of hope caged with
    despair,
begins to glimmer into the brightening light of dawn.
My chains fall from me – the prison doors swing open –
O my soul's become a diamond, glittering in the
    radiance of the rising sun –
moving upwards along its beams, back to the source of light!
Our years of suffering were the proper time for tears.
Now all suffering's over. Dry your eyes. Come. What is
    there to fear?
I see my Death approaching – he's wondrous – beautiful –
    an archangel, smiling.
He is a healer, come to comfort me, to be my truest friend.
Sweet Death will enfold me in his raven wings – covering
    my shame.
My earthly crown was a crown of sorrows – he will set
    a celestial crown upon my head.
The majesty in which he will dress me owes nothing to
    this world.
Melville?
Do not kneel, dear companion. After so many years, they
    allow you to return!
Now I have the comfort of a good old friend – one of
    my faith.
You shall witness my heavenly coronation – for that's what
    it shall be.

She helps him up and embraces him.

I thank God for you, Melville. It's a sad thing to die among
   strangers.
Now give me your word: when I am dead do not stay in
   England.
Go to my brother, Henri of France. He will welcome you.
   All of you.
You must not linger here – mocked and scorned –
to sink down under the jibes and jeers
of those who celebrate my death in drunken holiday.
Burghley's falsehoods have made a painted monster of me.
I have no doubt I shall be burned in effigy.
But you, sir – and you all – know the truth of Mary Stuart.

To her women:

They're returning my possessions. Ah, the vain treasures
   of this world!
I leave everything to you – my wardrobe – my pearls.
You're young enough to value such finery.
Margaret. These are for you. Never think I blame you
   for your husband's disloyalty.
He's a weak man – they must have forced him to it.
Treasures mean little to my Hannah. I embroidered this
   scarf for you.
When the time comes, bind my eyes with it. This last service
   I ask –
It must be done by you, and you alone.

Kennedy
Would you break my heart, child?

Mary
I'll wring it a little but it will not break. You will be proud
   of me –
and innocent pride strengthens the heart.

Kennedy
O God!

Mary
Come to me – all of you. A last farewell. So – so.

They kneel and kiss her hands, weeping.

Farewell, farewell. Forever, farewell!

She quickly turns from them. All except **Melville** *go out.*

Mary

I'm leaving my worldly affairs in good order, Melville.
No man will be the poorer for my passing.
My one remaining fear . . .
O my trembling soul – poised ready for flight –
feels a new power surge into in its unfolding wings –
But one thing – this one thing weighs my spirit to the earth –
    and such a thing . . .
O sir . . .

Melville

Tell me, My Lady.

Mary

I'm standing before you now, my faithful servant –
but almost before the sound of my words dies away
I shall stand before my Redeemer.
How may I face Him unconfessed? My sins lie heavy in my
    breast –
I am denied a priest of my own Church,
and I will not receive the sacrament from a Protestant.
I wish to die in a state of grace – I long for the comforts
    of the true faith.

Melville

Set your mind at rest.
Heaven accepts such longing in your heart as a sacrament.

Mary

Longing's not enough!
God was made man upon this earth –
He left us His divinity in the rites of Holy Church –
the means by which we may ascend to Him in heaven.
If this is not so, what need have we sinners of priests or
    Church?
When I receive the Host, Christ's presence is real – so real
    to me!

Facing what I must face – think what strength I'd have if
　　My Saviour was at my side –
If the confession of my faith made me sure of Him!
Here in my prison they shut Christ out.

Melville

Shut Him out! How can any man do that?
God who strikes water from the living rock –
makes flowers spring from a carved wooden staff –
can set up His altar in this prison house . . .
Or turn the wine in this cup –

He takes it from the table.

　– into His redeeming blood.

Mary

In the hands of a priest He would.

Melville

But when the heart so longs for grace – as does your own –
that's when God works His miracles.
Lady, I am a priest.
So that I may hear your last confession, and pronounce
　　your absolution,
I have taken holy orders, in Rome.

He bares his head.

Look. The body of Christ – blessed by the Holy Father.

He reveals the Host in a golden pattern.

Mary

In former times my steward knelt to me.
Now he has entered the service of the King of Heaven,
　　I gladly kneel to him.

Melville

In nomine Patris † et Filii † et Spiritus † Sancti.
Ne reminiscaris, Domine, delicta nostra vel parentum nostrorum,
　　neque vindictam sumas de peccatis nostris.
Mary, Queen of Scotland, search your heart. Before your
　　Maker confess your sins.

Mary

The truth in me I'll open – to you, and to God.

In my imprisonment, hatred and envy have almost gnawed away my heart.

My cries for forgiveness were cries for vengeance –

I could not forgive those who trespassed against me.

Melville

As you look upon death at your enemies' hands, do you repent this sin?

Do you, in your heart of hearts, forgive those enemies?

Mary

I do. I forgive them, as God will pardon me.

Melville

What other sin weighs down your soul?

Mary

The deadly sin of lust.

I gave my willing body to a faithless, hollow man.

I was punished in his betrayal.

Melville

Do you repent this sin?

Have you learned flesh is corruptible?

Do you desire only the incorruptible joys of heaven?

Mary

I have – I do.

No lesson has been harder, nor proved more bitter.

But I have learned no momentary, worldly bliss can match the joys of heaven.

Melville

What other sin?

Mary

My greatest. A sin of omission.

Though I have confessed it – and by harshest penance been absolved –

it still weighs leadenly upon my fluttering soul.

I mean the killing of my husband, Lord Darnley.

I looked away while they murdered him – and did nothing.

> If God has forgiven me this sin, why has the guilt of it
> never left my thoughts?

Melville

> What else is unconfessed?

Mary

> Nothing. God knows I have searched my heart.

Melville

> Leave no doubt unconcealed. Perpetual impenitence offends
> the Holy Spirit.

Mary

> I've hidden nothing.

Melville

> What of the crimes of which you stand accused?
> Your secretaries, Kurl and Nau, have sworn you plotted to
> kill Elizabeth.
> Heaven can forgive even this, but only if you confess it,
> and repent it.

Mary

> Upon my soul, I've no more to confess.

Melville

> I caution you, Lady – do not equivocate with heaven.
> Never believe you can satisfy God with partial truths.
> Perhaps, as in the murder of your husband, you looked
> away –
> had guilty knowledge of conspiracy – hoping it would
> succeed
> without your aid in it? Such silent acquiescence will bring
> you to the fires of hell.
> Confess, repent, and be absolved.

Mary

> I confess I wanted freedom, but never at the cost of
> Elizabeth's life.
> I have been party to no plot against her.
> Never have I hoped for, spoken for, nor contemplated
> her murder.

Melville

Then your secretaries lied to the Privy Council?

Mary

I will answer before my God, and so must they.

Melville

Then you will lay an innocent head upon the block?
Are you most sure of that?

Mary

I'll die an innocent –
As my husband did. Perhaps it's heaven's earthly
    punishment –
the means by which my soul returns to Christ.

Melville

Innocent blood washes clean the guilt of bloodshed.
Our crimes, absolved on earth, cannot plead against us
    before the throne of heaven.
Now, by the power vested in me to loose, or bind,
I absolve you from all sin.

*Absolve, quaesumus, Domine, animam famuli tui Maria ab omni
    vinculo delictorum: ut in resurrectionis Gloria inter Sanctos et
    electos tuos resuscitatus respiret. Per Christum Dominum nostrum.*
Amen.

Mary

Amen.

Melville

In nomine Patris † et Filii † et Spiritus † Sancti,
extinguatur in te omnis virtus diaboli per impositionem manuum
    nostrarum, et per invocationem omnium sanctorum Angelorum,
    Archangelorum, Patriarcharum, Prophetarum, Apostolorum,
    Martyrum, Confessorum, Virginum, atque omnium simul
    Sanctorum. Amen.

Mary

Amen.

Melville

As you believe, so may your soul find heaven.

He takes the Host from the pattern.

> *Ecce Agnus Dei, ecce tollit peccata mundi.*
> *Corpus Domini nostri Jesu Christi custodiat animam tuam in vitam aeternam.* Amen.

She receives the Host. He takes the cup of wine from the table, prays silently over it.

> *Sanguis Domini nostri Jesu Christi custodiat animam tuam in vitam aeternam.* Amen.

He offers it to her. She hesitates, then declines it with a gesture.

Receive the cup! The Pope himself allows it.
At the point of your death he grants the highest sacrament –
Christ's mystery – permitted only to priests and kings.

She takes it.

As here upon earth your body is one with Our Lord,
today you shall be with Him in Paradise.
All sin and guilt pass away. He shall wipe the tears from
    your eyes forever,
and He shall be with you, even unto the end of time.

† *Per Christum Dominum Nostrum.* Amen.

He puts down the cup. The noise of the guards is heard outside. He covers his head and goes to the door, while **Mary** *prays.*

Mary
> Amen. *Ave Maria, gratia plena: Dominus tecum: benedicta tu in mulieribus, et benedictus fructus ventris tui Jesus. Sancta Maria, Mater Dei, ora pro nobis peccatoribus nunc, et in hora mortis nostrae.* Amen.

Melville *lifts her up.*

Melville
> There are further trials. Are you strong enough to face
>   your enemies,
> and feel no surge of your former hatred for them?

Mary
> O I'll not slide back.

God has disabled all vengeful thoughts, that once held
power upon me.

Melville
Then prepare yourself.
Lord Burghley and the Earl of Leicester are here.

Enter **Paulet** *and* **Kent** *with guards, then* **Burghley** *with*
Richard Fletcher, *then finally* **Leicester**, *who stands aloof and*
avoids **Mary***'s gaze.* **Burghley** *occasionally looks at* **Leicester**,
trying to judge what he is thinking.

Burghley
Lady Stuart. I've come to hear your last requests.

Mary
Thank you, My Lord.

Burghley
My Queen has let it be known that nothing you require
shall be, unreasonably, withheld.

Mary
Sir Amyas Paulet has my will.
I am confident he will follow its provisions faithfully.

Paulet
You may be sure of it, Lady.

Mary
I must also ask that my household servants
be allowed safe conduct to the King, my brother-in-law.

Burghley
Granted.

Mary
And, since my body is to be buried in unsanctified ground,
I pray that they may take my heart with them for burial
in France.
Though France, in truth, never relinquished it.

Burghley
Granted.

Mary

Greet my sister, your Queen, from me.

Say that with all my heart I forgive her my death,

and beg her forgiveness for the violence of my language to her.

May God preserve her and exalt her reign.

Burghley

Dr Richard Fletcher, the Dean of Peterborough, has come to pray with you.

Mary

I am sorry he has wasted his journey. God has already granted me

the means to make my peace. Sir Amyas Paulet, I have been a great trouble to you –

I have not borne my imprisonment mildly, and, however unwillingly,

I have been the cause of your nephew, Mortimer's death.

O, I beg you, sir – let me hope you will not hate me for it!

Paulet (*through tears*)

God be with you, Royal Lady. And grant you His peace.

He kisses her hand.

The door opens. **Kennedy** *and the other ladies rush in, in great distress. Through the doorway can be seen the sheriff with his white staff, and officers of the guard.*

Mary

It's time for me to go. I see the sheriff has brought my death warrant.

I'll bid you farewell, My Lord, and friends. Hannah, you must come with me.

Burghley

I can't allow it.

Mary

Oh why? I cannot believe my sister would forbid me the assistance of my own people. Melville –

He hurries to her side.

Burghley
The scaffold's no place for women.

Embarrassed – realising what he has said:

I'll not have unseemly scenes of weeping and fainting –

Mary
You have my word, Hannah will not weep. For the love
of Christ, sir, do not separate us.
She took me in her arms when I was born – she'll lead
me by the hand up to my death.

Paulet
For God's sake, man, give way to her in this!

Burghley
Very well. Against my wiser judgement.

Mary
Now nothing of this word has power upon me.

She kisses her crucifix.

O my Redeemer – stretch wide Your blessed arms to
receive my soul!

*She takes opens her prayer book and starts to go, softly reciting the thirtieth
psalm.*

*In te speravi, Domine; dixi: Tu es Deus meus, in minibus tuis tempora
mea.*

She sways a little, then she fixes her eyes on **Leicester** *who steps
forward to support her, leans on his arm, then draws back from him.*

Mary
Leicester.
Once before you offered your support – swore you'd deliver
me from prison.
And now, as I leave captivity and the world, you keep your
word.
My heart finds no fault in you.

There's nothing of my old life left – nothing of this earth
    in my heart.

He's crushed.

You do me great good in drawing me out of this world –
    I am very glad to go.
Farewell, My Lord, and serve your mistress faithfully.
I pray she will not punish you for favours shown to me.
Allons donc!

She goes out, preceded by the sheriff and **Paulet***, and with* **Kennedy**
and **Melville** *at her side, then her ladies,* **Kent***,* **Burghley***, guards
and others. As she leaves she recites part of the sixteenth psalm.*

Mary
*Perfice gressus meos in semitis tuis, ut non moveantur vestigial mea:
inclina aurem tuam mihi, et exaudi verva mea: mirifica
misericordias tuas, qui salvos facis sperantes in te, Domine
Alleluja.*

Leicester *is left alone.*

Leicester
Why am I left alive! Mountains and hills fall upon me –
    earth open to receive me!
I cannot see her die! I cannot watch her die!

He flees.

We see **Mary** *calmly approaching the scaffold.*

Elizabeth*'s presence chamber. The Queen is in a state of extreme
nervousness.*

Elizabeth
Why don't they bring word? Someone must know what's
    happening.
The sun hangs motionless in the heavens and will not sink,
and every tedious minute lengthens into hours.
I'm in torment! Waiting, waiting, waiting. Pacing. Worrying.

Does she still live? Or am I free of her?
I dread her living, fear her dead, and dare not ask for news.

Enter **Page**.

Elizabeth

Has everyone deserted me? Where is Leicester? Where is Burghley?

Page

Majesty, the Earl of Leicester and Lord Burghley cannot be found –

Elizabeth

They're not in London?

Page

No, Madame. But where they are gone no one can tell me. They left the city by night and rode northward – nobody knows why or where –

Elizabeth

Then I'm England's Queen! Now God be praised! It must be over – over!

She paces back and forth in great excitement.

Go – quickly – fetch my – No! No, stay here.
She's dead, she's dead – praise God for it, she's dead – and no one dare blame me.
I'm trembling, trembling! My heart, my heart!
Is it sickness – is it fear? Pah! What is there to fear?
My fear lies buried in her grave – no one can say I sent her there.
They cannot say I killed her!
I must try and shed tears for her – tears, tears –
What are you doing here – who ordered you to wait? Fetch Davison – go quickly – fetch the secretary –

Enter **Shrewsbury** *in haste.*

Page

Majesty.

He bows out.

Elizabeth
Welcome, Lord Shrewsbury.

Shrewsbury
Majesty, I've come from the Tower. The news is bad, Lady,
bad as it could be –

Elizabeth
O! What news? Tell me – quickly, sir! Bad news –

Shrewsbury
Queen Mary's secretary – the Scotsman, Kurl – confesses
now
the statements he gave in evidence against his mistress
were all false.

Elizabeth
Never say so!

Shrewsbury
Rumours that the warrant has been signed have driven
him all but mad.
He rants, and prays, and tears his hair –
and blames his treachery on his fellow, Claude Nau –
who drew him into perjury, at Lord Burghley's prompting.

Elizabeth
No, no, no!

Shrewsbury
From the window in his prison cell he's proclaiming his
guilt to the world –

Elizabeth
Then stop him!

Shrewsbury
'I was secretary to the Queen of Scots!' he cries, 'My
perjury condemned her!'
O Madame, Madame –

Re-enter the **Page**, *with* **Davison**.

Elizabeth
But don't believe him – the ravings of a madman –

Shrewsbury
Lady, I beg you, withhold the warrant until we have looked
further into this business.
Madness or devilish conspiracy – the truth must be
searched out.

Elizabeth
It must, it must –

Shrewsbury
Thank God it's not too late!

Elizabeth
At your request, most loyal Lord,
I will hold back the sentence of my Parliament, and look
again into these sorry affairs.
No doubts, not so much as the shadow of a doubt, may
be allowed
to tarnish the brightness of the English crown.
Davison. Fetch me the warrant.

Davison (*as if poleaxed*)
The warrant? Majesty . . .

Elizabeth
Yesterday I placed it in your care.

Davison
My care?

Elizabeth
I signed it under pressure from the citizens.
Then gave it into your safe keeping – so that I might
consider at more leisure
what course I might pursue in this matter.
All this you know. And now I want it back.

Davison
I thought –

Elizabeth
You're not here to think, sir. What have you done with
my warrant?

Davison
My God, my God – have mercy on me!

Elizabeth
I hope, sir, you have not –

Davison
I'm lost – lost! I no longer have the warrant!

Elizabeth
What? Where –

Shrewsbury
Merciful heavens! –

Davison
It's in Lord Burghley's hands – he took it upon himself to –

Elizabeth
What – wretched man? Have I entrusted my kingdom's
honour to a fool – a fumbler?
Is this how you understand my clear commands?

Davison
My Lady, you wouldn't give me clear commands. I –

Elizabeth
Miserable slave! – will you make a liar of your Queen?
When did I order you to give Burghley the warrant?

Davison
You didn't, Majesty – your orders were confused – and
then I –

Elizabeth
O presumption!
Will you bend and twist my words to your own false
meaning? Do you dare!
If your malicious meddling produces some bloody outcome
your life is forfeit!

Lord Shrewsbury, you see how my authority's flouted –
my name's abused?

Shrewsbury
I do see –
this man must answer his incompetence before his peers.
I fear his failure in duty will expose Your Majesty's name
to the contempt of Europe, and History's harshest censure –

Enter **Burghley**, *who kneels.*

Burghley
Long live my most mighty sovereign – confusion to her
nation's traitors.
Royal Lady, your greatest enemy is dead.

Shrewsbury *covers his face.* **Davison** *wrings his hands.*

Elizabeth
Is she dead? Why?
Answer me, My Lord! Did you have authority for her
death from me?

Burghley
No, Madame. I had the warrant from Davison.

Elizabeth
And did Davison give it to you in my name?

Burghley
No. I cannot say he –

Elizabeth
And you never thought to come and know my mind in this?
This was no light matter, sir!
True – she deserved to die – the world cannot question
the warrant's legality –
But, sir, you know my nature is always to be merciful.
You have denied my poor sister access to the tenderness
of my heart –
stood in the sweet way I was going toward forgiveness.
For that I banish you the Court. Never let me see your face.

Exit **Burghley**. *Enter* **Page**.

Elizabeth
Davison.
You have carelessly betrayed a sacred trust.
Your life hangs by a thread – you will be tried before
  your peers.

Page
Guards!

Elizabeth
Remove him to the Tower.
O Shrewsbury! Faithful lord! – the only friend left to me –
the single honest voice in all my Council.
From this time your hand alone shall steer the ship of state.

Shrewsbury
You banish the most faithful of you counsellors,
and send a loyal servant to the Tower.
For me, great Queen, I must refuse the honours you'd
  heap on me –

Elizabeth
Shrewsbury! Surely you won't desert me. I am alone!

Shrewsbury
Pardon me, My Lady, I've grown old in your service.
I will no longer force this trembling hand to set England's
  Great Seal upon your Acts.

Elizabeth
Would you save my life, and then abandon me?

Shrewsbury
I saved your life. If only I could, as easily, preserve your
  soul!
God's blessing on your rule, and realm, Lady.
The source of your unrest is dead. Now you need fear
  nothing.
The world lies at your feet . . . Tread carefully.

He exits, followed by the **Page**, *who returns.*

Page

The Earl of Kent.

Enter **Kent**.

Elizabeth

Kent. Go and fetch the Earl of Leicester to me. Quickly!
Go!

Kent

Majesty, the Earl regrets he can no longer come to Court.
He is embarked for France.

Elizabeth *takes the blow, then masters herself, and gets to her feet –*
a mask of composure.

Elizabeth

I am alone. Leave us.